THE WAR OF 1812

NIAGARA STORY

VOLUME II

BY

ROBERT J. FOLEY

ILLUSTRATED BY

GEORGE BALBAR

THE HAUNTED PRESS

NIAGARA FALLS, ONTARIO

ISBN: 1-895528-02-X

Foley, Robert J. 1941-
   The War of 1812
   Niagara Story Volume II
   by Robert J. Foley
   Includes index

Illustrated by

Balbar, George

Printed in Canada by: Peninsula Press Limited, St. Catharines, Ontario

Bound in Canada by: John Van Huizen Book Binding, St. Catharines, Ontario

Canadian Cataloguing in Publication Data

Foley, Robert J., 1941-
   Niagara Story

Includes index

Contents: v. 1. Beginnings ---- v. 2. The War of 1812

ISBN 1-895528-00-3 (v. 1)   ISBN 1-895528-02-X (v. 2)

1. Niagara Peninsula (Ont.) - History. I. Title.

FC3095.N5F64 1994   971.338   C94-900997-0

F1059.N5F64 1994

Dedicated

To

My children

Michael and Catherine

My cup runneth over

The entire Niagara Story Series

is respectfully dedicated

To the late

George Seibel

and

His wife and editor

Olive Seibel

They are the yardstick by which all future Niagara historians will be measured.

Contents

PREFACE

This is Volume II in the Niagara Story Series, which is published Weekly in the St. Catharines Standard and in the Niagara Falls Review and Welland Tribune as Pioneer Days. In this book we follow the horrific events of the War of 1812 on our journey through the rich history of our pioneer ancestors. Young William Hamilton Merritt came of age during this conflict as he led his Provincial Dragoons against the American invaders.

The War of 1812 was a watershed in the history of our country. Our ancestors, through their actions in 1812-14 set us on an irreversible course toward nationhood. Although the book travels primarily within the Niagara Peninsula, it does take a number of detours to other venues from Michilimackinac to Chateauguay. It explores the diverse peoples that made up the combatants in this war that spawned a nation.

The success of the first volume of the series reinforces my belief that Canadians are interested in their history. The first printing sold out in less than three months. Many are discovering the excitement that is Canadian history.

This book is not meant to be a comprehensive history of the War of 1812. It is an attempt to bring the experiences of the participants to life in a series of snapshots of the events surrounding the conflict. To achieve this end I have included fictional narratives that can not be documented, however, the persons were there and their words and actions are plausible under the circumstances. To distinguish them from documented history they appear in italics so that the reader may easily tell the two apart.

If this series rekindles the readers interest in our history in some small way then we may judge it a success.

Bob Foley

Niagara Falls, Ontario

September 14, 1994

Acknowledgements

I would first like to acknowledge the men and women like William Hamilton Merritt, Laura Secord, Stephen Peer and the myriad other pioneers that are mentioned in this book. Their sacrifices made our nation possible.

I am grateful to those historians that have written on the war and the Niagara Region for the volumes of excellent materials made available to me in my research while working on the series. I would especially like to acknowledge the work of the late George Seibel in his history of the Portage Road. Together with his wife Olive he furnished accurate details of the people and places in Niagara. A special thanks to Don Graves of Ottawa for the work he did on the Battles of Chippawa and Lundy's Lane, which has put to rest many a controversy in the last couple of years. Don also gave me access to his unpublished thesis on Joseph Willcocks, which gave me some insights into the character and motives of this man.

Once again the wonderful illustrations of George Balbar bring the words to life. George's work is an intricate part of this project and much of its success can be laid at his doorstep.

Finally to the readers who made volume one such a success. Come let's continue our journey through the Halls of History.

CHAPTER ONE
THE GATHERING STORM

As the war clouds gathered over the Peninsula Major General Isaac Brock began agitating for an acceleration of the building and repair of the fortifications in Upper Canada. However, the Governor General, Sir George Prevost, was reluctant to spend funds on an area that he felt was indefensible and probably to be abandoned in the event of war. He did authorize Brock to raise flank companies in the militia regiments to be trained to a higher point of efficiency than the regular militia companies.

Brock ordered repairs to be made at Fort George, Fort Erie and Fort Malden at Amherstburg on the Detroit River wherever practical. Many improvements were made despite the shortage of funds. Improvisation was nothing new to military commanders posted in remote corners of the empire.

British strategy, in case of a North American war, held the defence of Halifax and Quebec City as its top priority. Prevost was prepared to abandon Upper Canada and Montreal should it become necessary. The only military significance of the area west of Kingston was the alliance with the western Indians with whom the British had been negotiating since the summer of 1808. Abandoning Upper Canada would at best, keep the Indians neutral and perhaps even drive them into the American camp.

In the meantime the Americans were doing their best to insure that the Indians would be eager to fight for the British cause. In late October 1811 William Henry Harrison marched with an army to drive the Indians from lands that the Shawnee under Techumseh had refused to allow settlers to occupy. On November 7th the battle of Tippecanoe destroyed Prophet's Town, the Pawnee capital, assuring that the Indians would be in the British camp if war came.

James Secord sat in the common room of

Bannister's Tavern, Queenston, with some of the local citizenry. Despite the problems with his mercantile business he was in good humour as he enjoyed a drink and some good conversation. The crop was in and it was a bumper year. Farmers would have grain to barter and pay their debts. It also insured a good supply of food stuffs for the coming winter.

Captain Samuel Hatt, who commanded one of the flank companies of the 5th Regiment of Lincoln Militia talked of the training that the flank companies were undergoing. He had spoken with General Brock himself at Fort George that very week on his way down to visit with his brother Richard, a major in the 1st Lincolns. He was particularly pleased with himself today for he had convinced his brother that in the case of war, which Samuel was sure was coming, he would join the 5th Lincolns so they could be together.

James Secord listened intently, envying Hatt's position. Secord had been a Lieutenant in the 1st Lincolns, but family and business pressures had forced him to resign his commission. If the war, which Samuel Hatt was so sure was just around the corner, came he would enlist as a private and fight for his home much as his father had fought in the American Revolutionary War some thirty years earlier.

Thomas Dickson, a native of Dumfrieshire, Scotland and a local merchant, remarked that war must be close. One of Brock's aides had come to him to get a line on his brother Robert who was living among the Sioux in the west. Dickson was sure that Brock wished his brother to use his influence to bring the western tribes into the war on Britain's side.

Isaac Brock sat in his study at York preparing a secret memorandum to Robert Dickson somewhere in the west. He was reportedly living with the Sioux Indians who called him Mascotapah, the red haired one.

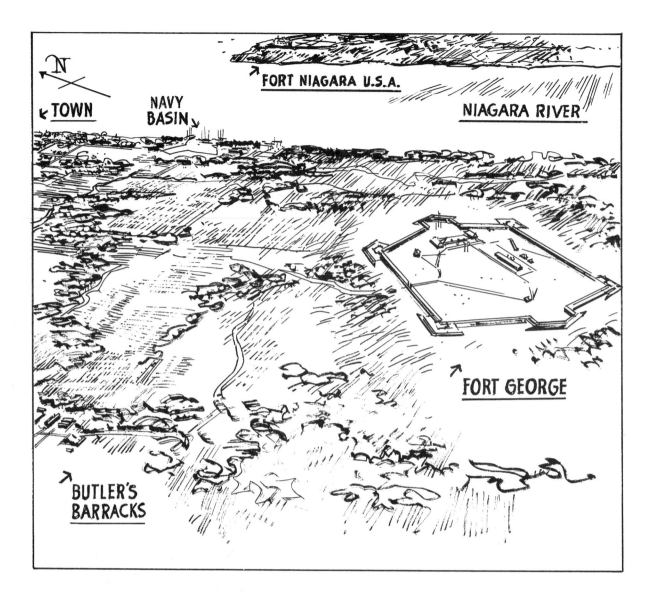

TOWN
NAVY BASIN
FORT NIAGARA U.S.A.
NIAGARA RIVER
FORT GEORGE
BUTLER'S BARRACKS

Brock knew that war was coming, yet he must be careful how he worded his communique lest it fall into the wrong hands. He did not want to leave himself open to a charge of inciting the Indians to war upon the United States. He deliberately couched his letter in Euphemisms. He wrote: "Confidential communication transmitted to Mr. Robert Dickson residing with the Indians near the Missouri,

Sir: As it is probable that war may result from the present state of affairs, it is very desirable to ascertain the degree of cooperation that you and your friends might be able to furnish, in case of such emergency taking place. You will be pleased to report with all practical expedition upon the following matters:

1st. The number of your friends that might be depended upon.

2nd. Their disposition toward us.

3rd. Would they assemble and march under your orders?

4th. State the succours you require and most eligible mode for their conveyance.

5th. Can equipment be procured in your country?

6th. An immediate direct communication with you is very much wished for.

7th. Can you point out in what manner that object may be accomplished?

8th. Send without loss of time a few faithful and confidential agents selected from your friends.

2

9th. Will you individually approach the Detroit frontier next spring? If so, state time and place where we may meet.

Memo: Avoid mentioning names in your written communications."

As much as was possible, with an overly cautious Prevost in command, Brock intended to be ready when the blow fell.

It is June 26, 1812. Major General Isaac Brock stands with the officers of the 41st Regiment at the gates of Fort George greeting the officers of the American garrison at Fort Niagara whom they have invited to dinner. The relationship between the two garrisons is amiable even friendly. The rankling over ship seizures and impressment seems remote in these frontier posts. After the usual comments about the late spring and its subsequent peril to this year's harvest, all go into the officer's mess to dine.

As the stewards begin to serve the main course an aide to Brock hurries into the room and hands him a slip of paper. He reads it, sits for a moment and then stands up and says, "Gentlemen, I have news. It seems that since the 11th instant, a state of war has existed between His Majesty and the Government of the United States."

An embarrassing silence followed until an officer of the 41st. stood and said, "With the general's permission might I suggest, in view of the fact that these gallant officers are our guests, that we continue our meal in fellowship and good cheer and leave the talk of war until after dinner."

The officers finished their dinner and the British saw their guests to the landing with hopes on both sides that hostilities would be short and that good relations might return before the summer was out. It was to be three bitter years before the last shot was fired in the War of 1812.

HISTORICAL NOTE: The story of the news of war being received at a mess dinner at Fort George is one of those legends that have come down to us through the years. It is repeated here for interest but may have no basis in fact.

CHAPTER TWO
WAR COMES TO NIAGARA

William Hamilton Merritt held the team's reins loosely as he drove toward the general store with his list of provisions in his pocket. He was anxious to get his business finished and get back to the farm that he ran for his father. The late spring made it impossible to get the crops planted until well past the usual date. Prospects for a repeat of the excellent harvest of the previous year seemed slim.

His mind thus occupied, Hamilton failed to see the young ensign of the 41st Regiment come galloping into Shipman's Corners until that young officer had pulled his horse up beside the wagon. With his excitement barely under control he informed Hamilton that war had been declared and that his father, Thomas, had been authorized to raise a troop of dragoons.

Provisions and farming were forgotten in an instant and Hamilton, a lieutenant in the militia, turned the team for home. Saddling his best horse he galloped off to Fort George. To this nineteen year old the prospects of adventure put all thoughts of danger from his mind. He was determined to report to General Brock himself and offer his services in any capacity the general thought fit.

At Fort George Brock welcomed young Merritt with enthusiasm. Brock knew the Merritts through his dealings with Hamilton's father, the sheriff of Niagara, and was impressed with the abilities of his son.

The Niagara Light Dragoons were being assembled and Brock gave Hamilton an appointment as lieutenant in that unit. He sent him off in command of a detachment of twenty troopers to mount a guard at Chippawa promising to send a further twenty when they become available. Brock was sure that the enemy would strike quickly and it was imperative to get patrols out as soon as possible.

Merritt's troop, augmented by additional reinforcements including Hamilton's cousin, Cornet William Merritt, patrolled the bank of the river from the mouth of the Chippawa south to a point where they met with the patrols from Fort Erie. They were on the alert for any unusual concentration of boats and troops that would signal an attack upon the province. Long days in the saddle took its toll on the citizen soldiers and when the expected invasion failed to materialize the early excitement gave way to the monotony of constant patrolling. They scanned the opposite river bank in vain for the enemy that should have been there.

On the same day that Hamilton Merritt received the news of the war, the word spread throughout the region. In Queenston, James Secord was contemplating his position. He had resigned his commission in the 1st Lincoln Militia a few years previously. He was now unsure as to how he could best serve in this war that no one wanted either on this side of the river or on the other. Communications between friends in Queenston and Lewiston had continued. Indeed, one local farmer was in the middle of negotiations to sell a cow to a farmer on the far bank and the two were confidently continuing to haggle.

James stepped into the street and headed for Bannister's Inn where the officers from Fort George were sorting out the militia for call up. He caught up to the farmer leading his cow down to the river where it was destined for Lewiston and its new American owner. Since there was no longer a ferry service on the river, he intended to row a boat across the water and swim her over. James wished him good luck and turned into Bannister's.

The inn's common room was filled with militiamen reporting or seeking an exemption from service. James approached a table where an harassed looking captain was sorting out a mountain of paper which James

4

to repel the invasion that must inevitably come, the Americans were discovering that they were not prepared for this war. The Militia was the bulwark of the American defense structure, a legacy of Jefferson who had a distrust of regular armies as corrupt and the instrument of kings. As the threat of war increased in 1811, however, the American government proposed to raise thirty-five thousand regular troops plus a further fifty thousand volunteers. It became quicklyapparent that the politicians were dreaming. The available supplies in arms and equipment kept this number well below the authorized total.

At the outbreak of war General William Hull, a Revolutionary War hero, moved toward Detroit with a force numbering two thousand men. This army consisted of sixteen hundred volunteers of the Ohio Militia and four hundred regulars. The British had a force of three hundred regulars and some militia at Fort Malden near Amherstburg to oppose the American troops destined for Detroit.

On the Niagara Frontier the American General, Stephen Van Rensselaer, a militia officer, was mustering a force of six thousand men. To oppose him Brock had twelve hundred regulars plus militia scattered over the frontier from Fort Erie to Niagara (Niagara-on-the-lake).

Things looked bleak for the Peninsula.

recognized as everything from muster rolls to requisitions for stores. Without looking up the captain directed him to an equally harassed lieutenant who in turn sent him to Ensign Peter Ball of the second flank company of the 1st Lincoln Militia Regiment. Ball greeted James and then sat in confusion not knowing whether he should be treated as a common soldier or an officer. James helped him out of his dilemma by immediately enlisting as a private. A relieved ensign gave him his instructions as to muster days and training. Since he had already taken the oath of allegiance, James was allowed to go home. As he left the inn he met a young farmer who was reporting for duty. He was in a state of great excitement. He remarked that they were in for a great adventure. James had heard enough stories from his uncle and other veterans of the Revolutionary War to know that the great adventure was really a journey into terror alternating with periods of sheer boredom.

As the British made feverish preparations

CHAPTER THREE
MICHILIMACKINAC

While the peninsula prepared for war, Robert Dickson was acting on Isaac Brock's communique and gathering the western tribes for the coming conflict. He moved his force in small groups to the British outpost at St. Joseph's Island. The outpost was a dilapidated blockhouse with a few old six pounder guns to defend it. The garrison consisted of members of the 10th Royal Veterans Battalion, a newly formed unit made up of veterans too old to fight, but thought to be suitable for garrison duty.

Captain Charles Roberts, a veteran of 20 years in the army, found the battalion so debilitated by a lifetime of drunkenness as to be useless even for the simple duties assign to it. Subsequently, the voyageurs, Dickson's western Indians and the local Chippewas and Ottawas, under John Askin Jr., made up the bulk of Roberts' offensive power. Askin was the keeper of the Indian stores at St. Joseph's.

Meanwhile the American commander at Michilimackinac, Lieutenant Porter Hanks, knew that something was afoot. The increased traffic of canoes heading for the British post loaded with warriors made him very uneasy. The coolness of once friendly Chippewa and Ottawa chiefs added to his sense of apprehension. It had been nine months since he had heard from Washington, so, unlike his British counterpart, he was totally ignorant of the declaration of war by his government.

If Hanks was forgotten by his government Roberts was not blessed with the problem. After the initial order from Brock, which he received on July 8, that the war was on and that he should act accordingly. He received another communique on July 12 advising him to sit tight. The Governor General, Sir George Prevost, still hoped to avoid war and put a hold on all offensive operations.

The Indians and voyageurs gathered at St. Joseph's Island were chafing for action. Roberts knew that he could not hold them for long and they would soon begin to drift away. July 15 brought the dispatch he had been praying for. Brock stretched the Governor General's orders to the limit. He advised Roberts to: "adopt the most prudent measures either of offense or defense which circumstances might point out." Roberts was free to act.

On the morning of the 16th his multi-hued army gathered to the fifes and drums to embark on their mission to Michilimackinac. The red tunics of the Veterans Battalion boarding the "Caledonia" contrasted with the capotes, kerchiefs and sashes of the 180 voyageurs of the Northwest Company in their Mackinac boats. Following in 70 birch bark canoes was Dickson with his 50 Sioux adorned with feathers and the Chippewa with their coal blackened faces, shaved heads and bodies smeared with pipe clay. Big Canoe, the famous one eyed chief, led his two dozen Winnebago; Tomah, head chief of the Menominee, brought 40 warriors; and the 30 Ottawa followed the Metis trader Amable Chevalier. 300 Warriors in all eagerly set out to do battle with the Long Knives, as the western Indians called the Americans.

The convoy traveled quickly, hoping to reach their objective before dawn. At midnight a lone birch bark canoe came paddling out of the darkness. Michael Dousman, a fur trader from Michilimackinac, was going to St. Joseph's to find out what was going on. As a sometimes partner of the leaders of the voyageurs and Indians, he greeted Dickson and Askin as old friends and was treated in kind by them. Although Dousman was an American Militia commander his main preoccupation was fur trading. He was concerned for the safety of the civilian population of the island and told Roberts all he needed to know

regarding defenses, hoping to protect the people from the wrath of the warriors present.

Dousman agreed to quietly wake the town and herd them into the old distillery where they could be guarded by regulars. He promised not to alert the garrison. At 3 in the morning, with the help of Dousman's oxen, the British landed and dragged two six pounders into position above the fort. Dousman then went from door to door quietly moving the civilians to safety.

Hanks awoke to the drum roll of reveille and peered down on the village. He knew immediately that something was wrong. No smoke curled from the chimneys, no early morning bustle broke the stillness. A lone figure ran up the slope toward the fort. The garrison surgeon's mate, Sylvester Day, repor-

ted that British redcoats and Indians had landed and three of the more prominent citizens were held as hostages.

Hanks immediately mustered his command and manned the walls. He then spotted the six pounders on the slope above him as well as the redcoats of the regulars. What disturbed him the most was the painted bodies of the native warriors. The dreaded word massacre flitted through his mind. A flag of truce suddenly appeared from the village and a British officer, accompanied by the hostages, demanded the surrender of the fort. Hanks needed no convincing, he agreed to turn over the fort and the island.

The terms given the Americans were simple. Anyone not prepared to take the oath of allegiance to the king must leave. All troops were paroled to their homes and were not to participate in the war until properly exchanged.

The battle was over without a shot being fired. Roberts' fears as to the deportment of his Indian allies proved unfounded. He wrote to Brock: "It is a circumstance I believe without precedent, as soon as they heard the capitulation was signed they all returned to their canoes, and not one drop either of man's or animal's blood was spilt..."

Young John Askin was convinced that the Hanks surrender prevented an Indian massacre. He wrote: "It was a fortunate circumstance that the fort capitulated without firing a single gun, for had they done so, I firmly believe not a soul of them would have been saved...I never saw so determined a set of people as the Chippewas and Ottawas were. Since the capitulation they have not drunk a single drop of liquor, nor killed a fowl belonging to any person (a thing never known before) for they generally destroy everything they meet."

Dickson's allies were not so easy to mollify. They complained to him that they had been cheated out of a fight. To help satisfy them a number of cattle were turned loose for them.

The capture of Michilimackinac assured the British of the active support of the western Indians. It was also the foreshadowing of things to come in the opening year of the War of 1812.

CHAPTER FOUR

THE PATHS OF GLORY

The mood of the Peninsula pioneers was sombre as the month of July drew to a close. Word from friends on the American side told of a steady buildup of troops, both regular and militia, at Lewiston and Buffalo. It seemed only a matter of time before Niagara fell to the enemy.

Those of loyalist stock would grimly defend their homes regardless of the odds, while some later arrivals, many from the United States, were reluctant to get involved. Some others welcomed the prospect of Upper Canada becoming a part of the United States and were quite open in expressing their willingness to help the invaders.

The Merritt family was not immune to this disaffection. Hamilton's cousin William Merritt spoke openly of the inevitability of an American victory. Even though he held a commission as Cornet in his Uncle Thomas' Niagara Light Dragoons, William feared the prospect of being caught on the losing side. (See historical note.)

The village of Queenston was buzzing with excitement with the news of General Brock's intended march to the Detroit front. A group of sixty volunteers was marching to join the flank companies of the 5th Lincolns and a detachment of the 41st Regiment of Foot among others. They were to meet the main body at Port Dover on Lake Erie. The column of volunteers moved off along the Portage Road swinging west at Lundy's Lane for the long march to Port Dover where boats would convey them the rest of the way to Amherstburg.

Spirits were high among the volunteers. Brock ended all talk of an easy American victory by taking the offensive. After many nights on the road, one spent camped at Brown's Bridge, the volunteers finally reached Port Dover only to find that they had missed the main body. Brock and the main column had left the previous day. Undaunted the volunteers moved off along the shore line hoping to catch up.

Major Richard Hatt of the 5nd Regiment of Lincoln Militia watched the preparations for the departure from Port Dover. The boats that had been expect to be here did not materialize and the staff was in a panic rounding up replacements. His regiment's morale was high despite the rain and lack of equipment. Their confidence in General Brock's ability to lead them to victory was unwavering.

The troops left Port Dover on the 9th of August in ten dilapidated boats and the men soon became exhausted from bailing. To add to the hardship the largest vessel in the flotilla, the one hundred ton schooner "Nancy", had to be manhandled over the narrow neck of sand at Long Point. This backbreaking exercise took all of the boat crews plus the troops who cursed and coaxed the ship to the deep water on the other side.

A sudden rainstorm forced them into Port Talbot where Hatt was pleasantly surprised to find sixty volunteers from Queenston waiting for them. A rousing cheer went up from them as they hove into sight and the main column answered in kind. All that day they lay on the open beach as the rain pelted down, soaking them throughly. Everything was wet; even the salt pork and hard biscuits were soggy from the damp conditions.

The next morning dawned overcast although the rain had stopped. Major Hatt could feel the beginnings of blisters as he squelched along in his wet boots. A veteran officer of the 41st told him to save his dry socks until they were in the boats and could take off their boots to give them an opportunity to dry out. Major Hatt felt that he would never be dry again.

The day continued overcast as the boats

set out. Hatt's wet uniform began to itch. The cold breeze off of the lake made him dream of his warm bed back in Queenston.

A sudden dropping of sails and the ensuing confusion brought him back to reality. Word filtered back that the general's boat had struck a submerged rock and was stuck fast. The boats idled about for an hour, the crews using their oars just to maintain some sort of position. The men in Richard Hatt's boat, their feet blistered and sore from their wet boots, teeth chattering from the damp cold of the lake, could not have been more miserable. Their heads shot up, however, when a sudden cheer exploded from the front of the column of boats. The cheer was picked up by each boat in succession. General Brock, in full uniform, had jumped into the water and the entire boat

followed, freeing the grounded vessel. He then broke open his case of spirits and offered everyone on board a drink. Major Hatt cheered with the rest and suddenly sore feet and wet clothes did not seem so bad. The troops straggled into Amherstburg, exhausted from rowing, on August 12th at eight p.m.

William Hamilton Merritt rode into the homestead for a well deserved rest after constantly patrolling the Niagara River since war was declared. He was only there a short time, however, when an urgent message was received from General Brock's headquarters indicating that Brock was going to take personal command at Amherstburg. He ordered Merritt to take his troop of dragoons and maintain the line of communication between Amherstburg and York. Brock added a postscript to the order that must have pleased Merritt to no end. The general wrote: "I am well pleased with your exertions, and wish you to see more active service."

Merritt gathered his weary troop and rushed off to execute his mission. At this point in the campaign Merritt's dragoons were without distinctive uniforms and at one stop for refreshments some American sympathizers mistook them for American cavalry. *One raised his glass, "To the Republic." Merritt raised his glass without a word, his slight hand signal stopping the protests of his men before they were uttered.*

"If you fellows need any help we'll be happy to oblige, the sooner you beat the British the better as far as we're concerned." All nodded in agreement with their spokesman. "We know the country here abouts and are willing to supply you with information, provided you remember us when the wars over of course," he said winking knowingly at Merritt.

Merritt drew his pistol and said, "Lieutenant William Hamilton Merritt of his Majesty's Niagara Light Dragoons at your service, gentlemen." A groan went up from the crowd as the dragoons surrounded them.

Merritt arrested a dozen of them and conveyed them to Fort George before resuming his ride. This delayed his arrival at Amherstburg until the day after the capture of Detroit. Brock awarded him the Detroit Medal nevertheless.

HISTORICAL NOTE: William Merritt, cornet in the Niagara Light Dragoons and cousin of William Hamilton Merritt, eventually deserted to the enemy.

THE CAPTURE OF DETROIT

Amherstburg was a beehive of activity as preparations for the coming campaign were completed. With the arrival of General Brock offence became the watch word of the day. All those who attended the war council were for caution except Brock himself, Colonel Robert Nicol, Quartermaster General of the militia and Tecumseh, the Shawnee Chief. Brock, the commander, got his way and the fate of Upper Canada was to be decided by daring and bluff before the walls of Fort Detroit.

William McCay of York stood with the other men of the flank company of the 2nd York Militia as they were issued the scarlet uniform coatees of the 41st Regiment of Foot. The 41st had received a new shipment from Quebec to replace their threadbare uniforms. The plan was for some of the militia to take on the appearance of regulars thus deceiving an already nervous General William Hull commanding the American forces.

The coat that McCay received was shabby. The sleeves were too short and it was rather snug in the shoulders, but he looked and felt like a regular. He would march directly behind the 41st, that is all that mattered to him.

The scene in the streets of Amherstburg was chaotic. Troops prepared to march to Sandwich across from Detroit. Indians roamed in groups preparing in their own way for what was to come. The excitement denied McCay any sleep that night.

Brock's strategy for the coming battle played a lot on the American fear of Indians. A fake letter, intercepted by the Americans, purportedly for the commander at Michilimackinac asked him to send five thousand Indians to assist in the campaign. The very thought of this many warriors would play havoc with Hull's already fragile mental state.

As his troops gathered at Sandwich, Brock ordered the construction of a secret battery containing an 18 pounder, two 12 pounder guns and a couple of mortars for the forthcoming bombardment. With an audacity only the British could muster, Brock sent two aides to demand the surrender of Detroit, which was defended by a larger force than Brock could put in the field. The aides played on Hull's fear of an Indian massacre, telling him that in the case of a battle they were not sure that they could control their Indian allies. Hull refused the terms and prepared to defend his post. The bombardment began.

The first roar of the cannons caught William McCay by surprise and he jumped up as the first balls flew across the river. The Americans soon replied and the cannonade continued well into the night. He gathered with many others and watched with a mixture of awe and fear as the Indians began their war dance. Some were smeared with vermilion, while others streaked their bodies with blue clay and still others were tattooed from head to foot with black and white markings. The hair on McCay's neck stood on end as he watched the warriors, naked except for their breechcloths, leaping and dancing by the light of a huge camp fire. Six hundred warriors worked themselves up for the coming battle. It was a sight he would never forget. Sometime during the night the Indians slipped across the river and took up positions in the woods before the fort.

The sky began to lighten as McCay joined the others to embark in the boats for the crossing of the Detroit River. He suddenly realized that it was Sunday and his family would be getting the chores done before going to church. It was strange, but, this was the first time he had thought of them since leaving York. For the first time a sense of uneasiness came over him.

As the sun crept over the horizon he caught sight of Brock, resplendent in his full uniform, standing in the lead boat. The sight left McCay breathless and calmed the butterflies that were beginning to form in his stomach. After all, if the general can stand up in full view of the enemy it couldn't be all that dangerous. At that moment he spotted a figure riding a white mustang at the landing place. It was Tecumseh and his chiefs. The enemy was nowhere in sight and the landing was accomplished unopposed.

The troops formed up in column with McCay's company marching directly behind the regulars of the 41st Foot. McCay could see two guns by the fort gates that covered the road up which they must march. A veteran told him they were 24 pounders and one round shot could mow down a file of twenty-five men like that, emphasizing the point with a loud snap of his fingers.

The column stepped off and McCay could not keep his eyes off of the two guns. The gunners stood by them at attention with smoke from their slow matches curling into the air as if sniffing out their presence. It seemed to him that they were marching right into the mouths of those guns and none would escape that first, deadly salvo. His stomach tightened in anticipation. He had an almost overwhelming urge to run, but, at that moment, he caught sight of Brock riding to the front of the column and his fit of panic passed.

McCay tried not to look at the guns. The tension became almost unbearable. He wished they would fire and get it over with.

Just when he thought he could stand it no longer the column veered off into a ravine and safety, out of sight of those threatening muzzles.

On wheeling his troops into the protective ravine Brock commandeered the farmhouse of William Forsyth as his headquarters and prepared the second phase of his plan of attack. He ordered Tecumseh to have his warriors lope out of the woods into an open meadow and back into the woods. They repeated this manoeuvre three times. The six hundred warriors were reported to Hull as fifteen hundred.

Brock moved cautiously fifty yards in front of his troops to reconnoitre his position when an American officer suddenly appeared bearing a flag of truce. The battle ended before it began. Detroit surrendered without a fight. The entire western front fell to the British without a shot being fired.

CHAPTER SIX
THE CALM BEFORE THE STORM

While Brock was winning a major victory at Detroit the ever cautious Sir George Prevost, the Governor General, was attempting to contain the war. He felt that if the British could avoid antagonizing the Americans that peace would come quickly.

On the day that Hull signed the instrument of surrender at Detroit, a British officer crossed the Niagara River to Lewiston under a flag of truce with a copy of a letter to the American commander, General Dearborn, proposing an armistice. The Americans were overjoyed for, despite numerical superiority, they feared an attack by the British and now had time to bring up reinforcements and supplies.

News of the armistice was welcomed in Queenston too. Few in the village and surrounding countryside wanted a war. They knew that a prolonged conflict would set them back years in their quest to better the lives of their families.

The armistice was to commence on August 20th and to be terminated on four days notice by either side. Even before the date, flags of truce were streaming across the river with letters and greetings among friends. One letter in particular was a cause of many a good laugh on both sides of the river. The farmer who had sold his cow to the American farmer as the war had begun wrote that the cow was back in his possession. Being a loyal British cow, she had swum back to the Canadian side. The farmer assured the buyer that he would keep her for him until the end of hostilities.

Thursday, August 27th, in the early afternoon, a rider came galloping into Queenston in an air of great excitement. James Secord did not have long to wonder at his mission for over the crest of the escarpment, straggling over a half mile of the Portage Road, stumbled the remnants of William Hull's army of Detroit.

The prisoners had been landed at Fort Erie and marched overland to prevent the Americans from attempting a rescue on the way down the river to Chippawa. It was also meant to cow the New York State Militia who could see the line of ragged men staggering along the river road.

The story of the victory at Detroit quickly spread among the villagers bringing cheers and celebrations. One look at the dispirited, gaunt figures of the American prisoners soon brought all thoughts of revelry to an end.

The column halted in the trees on the heights for a rest and Laura Secord and many of the other women of the village went among them with fresh water. James and some of the members of his company of the 1st Lincolns took over guard duty while the escort went into the village for refreshments.

James was struck by the misery he saw there. Many were shoeless and wore home-spun trousers much the same as those of his own company. What haunted him for days after was their eyes. In them he saw, for the first time, defeat. Not the defeat suffered after a hard fought battle, but the defeat of an army that had not fired a shot.

As the column staggered out of Queenston, volunteers, who had accompanied Brock to Detroit, came marching into the village to renewed cheering and much back slapping. Some gathered around William McCay of York admiring his scarlet coatee and stovepipe Shako that he had worn in the battle. After he had told the story of his adventures. many times over he headed for his unit's camp on the heights. He stopped long enough to speak to James Secord whom he encountered outside the latter's home as he came from guarding the American prisoners. He had been in a real campaign and lived to tell about it, but the realities of war were beginning to tarnish the excitement that had started his march from

York such a short time ago.

Brock boarded the schooner "Chippewa" on Lake Ontario for the trip back to York. He was much pleased with his victory at Detroit and was congratulating himself when the Provincial Schooner "Lady Prevost" approached and fired a seventeen gun salute. Her young commander came aboard and handed Brock his dispatches giving him his first knowledge of the armistice.

Brock's elation melted. He couldn't contain his anger at the news. His plan to follow up his victory by rolling up the American forces in New York from Buffalo to Sackett's Harbor while the enemy was unbalanced and short of supplies was undone, not by powder and shot, but by the scratch of a pen.

Brock had hoped for a quick victory in Canada so he could return to Britain and hence to the battlefields of Europe where glory and promotion would surely be his. He already was in receipt of permission to leave, but his sense of duty would not let him abandon his command at that critical juncture.

Despite the disappointment of the armistice Brock could not help but be pleased with the Detroit campaign. The American claim that his victory was pure luck angered Brock. He believe in thorough, meticulous planning, nothing left to chance. Although he admitted that he had taken a desperate gamble he asserted that victory was the result of a careful weighing of the pros and cons and then executing a well thought out plan.

Brock's reception at York and later at Kingston was beyond his expectations. Crowds gathered and he received a hero's welcome wherever he went. At Kingston he replied with humility, giving praise to the York and Lincoln Militia who had accompanied him. He stated that their presence induced him to attack Detroit as he did.

Brock returned to Fort George on September 6th in time for the end of the armistice. The Americans were heavily reinforced and he expected an invasion immediately. He wrote: "The enemy will either turn my left flank which he may easily accomplish during a calm night or attempt to force his way across under cover of artillery."

His Detroit victory had paid another dividend. Five hundred Mohawk warriors under John Norton cast off their neutrality and joined the British cause. They arrived at Niagara to reinforce the regulars and militia gathered there.

The armistice came to an end on September the 8th and both sides braced for the invasion they believed was coming. Nothing happened, for General Stephen Van Rensselaer, commanding the New York State Militia on the Niagara, hesitated to commit himself and Prevost shackled Brock in a vain hope that the war could be finished quickly without further bloodshed.

When harvest time approached Brock released most of the militia to attend their farms instructing them to be ready for recall at a moments notice. Everyone settled down to await the next move. As September gave way to October the clouds of war began to overshadow the uneasy peace that prevailed in the Niagara Peninsula.

THE BATTLE OF QUEENSTON HEIGHTS

A cold drizzle fell incessantly in the early morning hours of October 13, 1812. The sentry, from the 5th regiment of Lincoln Militia, standing guard at the edge of the village estimated the time at about 3 a.m. He prayed that the next hour would pass quickly and that his relief would be on time. The chill penetrated everything and he fought the urge to curl up among the trees to try to get warm, but he knew that sleep would follow quickly bringing the inevitable punishment for sleeping on duty.

As he dreamed of getting out of his wet clothes and seeking the relative warmth of his blanket, a noise caught his attention. He turned to see shadowy figures coming up from the river. At first he thought it was his relief coming early, then the faint sound of boats being pulled up on shore reached his ears above the roar of the river. The Americans had landed.

The sentry, whether out of fear or presence of mind, turned and ran back to the main guard to raise the alarm without firing his musket. Had he done so the enemy would have been alerted to their having been discovered.

Captain James Dennis, commanding the Grenadier Company of the 49th Regiment of Foot, immediately gathered up his company along with a few Lincoln militiamen and headed down into the village. Dennis found the enemy still landing troops and in much confusion. He formed up his men and gave the order to fire. The predawn solitude was shattered by a ragged volley of musketry.

The affects of this well timed onslaught were devastating. The American commander, Colonel Solomon Van Rensselaer, was struck by six bullets and several officers were either killed or wounded. This initial volley signaled the American batteries in Lewiston to begin bombarding the British positions. They con-

centrated their efforts on the single 18 pounder gun in the redan located half way up the heights, which began to lob shot down on the boats as they attempted to cross the river.

The batteries soon shifted their six guns to the small group of defenders forcing them to seek shelter among the houses close to the river. The house of Robert Hamilton was soon reduced to rubble by the American cannonade.

Captain John Chisholm's company of the 2nd Regiment of York Militia was alerted by the rattle of musketry and subsequent crash of artillery from Queenston, a mile to the south. The Yorks were guarding the 24 pound battery at Vrooman's Point and they immediately took up defensive positions as the gunners put their piece into action. Although it was still very dark the gunners could make out the boats in the water as the flash from the guns lit up the surrounding area. They began a bombardment that was to continue for most of the day.

Laura Secord awoke with a start as the American invasion began. The roar of the cannon in the Redan battery told her that the entire force was engaged. She also realized that her house was in the line of fire as the Americans attempted to put the redan battery out of commission.

Laura's husband James was with his company of the 1st Lincoln Militia so she was on her own. She immediately packed up her children and, skirting the heights, headed down the St. Davids Road to the farm of friends out of harm's way. As she marched along the road, chased by the sounds and sights of battle, she thought of her husband and the company he was assigned to. Would they see action? Would James be in danger? As Laura moved to safety, James Secord huddled with the rest of his company in the garden of Robert Hamilton's house.

18

Captain John Chisholm moved among his pickets at Vrooman's Point accompanied by the roar of their 24 pounder. He did not have to caution his men to keep a sharp eye for the sounds of battle had every man on the alert. A sudden challenge and a volley of musket fire sent him running to the river bank. A large boatload of American infantry was attempting to come ashore and the steady fire of his company was having a devastating effect on them. It turned out that the boat had missed its landing place and had been swept down river. A cry for quarter brought the order to cease fire and the Americans were taken prisoner. They were immediately sent toward Fort George carrying their wounded as best they could.

At Fort George Major General Isaac Brock was awakened by the sound of artillery from the south. He dressed and waited for some word from Queenston as he was convinced that this was a mere feint and the real attack would come elsewhere, perhaps right there at Niagara.

The steady cannonade finally convinced him that the threat was to Queenston and, riding his favourite horse, Alfred, he set out with his Provincial Aide de Camp, Lieutenant Colonel John Macdonell and his A.D.C. Captain John Glegg. He galloped toward Queenston leaving orders for the garrison to prepare to move at first light. Brock paused only at the Field House and Brown's Point to direct the militia units there to follow after him and he was off again riding toward the sound of the guns.

As the grey light of dawn streaked the eastern sky the weary men of the 49th Foot gave a cheer. Their general (Brock had risen from subaltern to colonel in the 49th) had arrived to lead them to victory. The stage was set for phase two of the Battle of Queenston Heights.

Upon riding into Queenston Brock acknowledged the cheers of his regiment and immediately rode Alfred up to the redan to reconnoitre the battlefield. As the panorama of the battalions of American troops awaiting embarkation in Lewiston unfolded itself Brock realized that this was the main thrust. He sent one of his aides scurrying back to Fort George and another to Chippawa to rush reinforcements forward.

A ragged cheer from behind the battery toward the crest of the heights made Brock turn around. He found himself staring at the charging form of American infantry. Captain John Wool of the 13th U.S. Infantry had discovered an old fisherman's path up the heights and had managed to get to the top undetected. The British gunners just had time to break a ramrod off in the touchhole rendering the guns useless before Brock, leading Alfred by his reins, ordered the retreat into the village.

The situation was desperate. Brock felt that whoever controlled the heights controlled Upper Canada. Before the Americans could reinforce the redan position he was determined to recover it with a charge using two hundred men of the 49th Regiment and some militia.

Those men new to battle were numbed by the crash of cannon balls and falling masonry as they crouched in the garden of the Hamilton house, which lay in ruins from the bombardment. General Brock suddenly mounted his horse and call out, "Follow me, boys."

At a stone wall Brock dismounted and took cover. He turned to his troops and said, "Take a breath, boys, you will need it in a few moments." They all cheered their general's little joke and followed him over the wall. Among them, George Jarvis of York, a fifteen year old gentleman volunteer in the 49th, and James Secord of the 1st Lincoln Militia.

Slipping and sliding on the wet leaves that littered the ground, they joined the charge toward the redan. Jarvis could hear the musket balls snapping past his head. The man in front of him suddenly pitched backwards and nearly knocked him down. The charge was momentarily halted until the general bolted forward and the troops resumed their mad rush.

Jarvis soon found himself near the front of the pack as he concentrated on the brilliant uniform and plumed hat of General Brock. He saw a blurred image of an American marksman stepping from behind a tree about thirty paces away. He tried to shout a warning, but no words came. The musket spewed smoke and flame and Brock crumpled on his left side and lay still. Jarvis ran to his side inquiring if he were badly hurt, but one look told him that Brock was dead. Disheartened by the death of their commander, the 49th gathered up his body for the withdrawal back to the village. As they turned to leave James Secord spun and dropped to the ground in a hail of musket balls. Secord did not hear the retreating footsteps or the continuing sounds of battle that swirled around him.

At that moment two companies of York Militia arrived on the scene led by Brock's aide John MacDonell. He rallied the troops for another crack at the redan and with a cry of, "Revenge the general," seventy volunteers charged forward led by MacDonell on horseback.

George Jarvis was, again, in the forefront of the charge. As he struggled up the slope MacDonell's horse, struck by a musket ball, wheeled around and at that moment MacDonell fell to the ground. Jarvis and some others ran to help him up, but he had been shot in the back, a wound that proved fatal. The men reeled back before the onslaught of fire from the reinforced redan. Soon the heights and the village were in American

hands.

Victory was within the grasp of the Americans, but, problems loomed to frustrate the consolidation of their success. The New York State Militia, who had been clamouring for the invasion of Canada, looked with dismay at the wounded being ferried back across the river. They suddenly remembered that under the Constitution they were not required to serve outside the state. They refused to embark into the boats. Pleas, threats and questions of their manhood were of no avail.

Meanwhile Winfield Scott, now commanding the troops on the heights, waited in vain for reinforcement and resupply. He found his force dwindling as some of the militiamen, who had crossed, began melting away.

As Scott struggled with his problems, command of the British forces devolved to Major-General Roger Sheaffe who would not repeat Brock's frontal assault. His force turn west before entering the village and gained the heights by way of a road to the west of Queenston. There he waited for the reinforcements from Chippawa before attempting an assault.

About 3 p.m. Sheaffe ordered the Indians commanded by John Brant, son of Joseph, and John Norton, a Scot adopted by the Mohawks, forward. He immediately began his own advance with the 41st Regiment and militia including the 1st Lincolns and the Niagara Light Dragoons.

Lieutenant William Hamilton Merritt held his horse in check as they waited for orders.

He glanced down the line where his father, Major Thomas Merritt, was conferring with General Sheaffe. The day had been a whirl of activity consummated by the mad gallop to Queenston and the report of the death of General Brock.

The Indians opened fire and Merritt could hear their war cries ringing through the woods. He knew that the American militia had a fear of Indians that bordered on paranoia and many had come into the lines waving white handkerchiefs begging for protection.

The battle ended quickly as Scott, low on ammunition and losing his force to desertions, surrendered his troops. Some militiamen, in a panic to escape the wrath of the British Indian allies, threw themselves into the river or on to the rocks below.

By late afternoon Laura Secord could no longer sit and wonder what had happened to her husband. When the sound of gunfire diminished enough she left her children and headed back to the village. The sight that greeted her brought tears to her eyes. The wounded of both sides lay everywhere, some in silence, others crying out for water or screaming with pain.

Where was James? She asked everyone she met, but none had seen him since that morning. He was not at home. She began to search among the dead and wounded in the area where he had last been in action. She despaired at ever finding him alive until, suddenly, there he was, lying not six feet from her. He was moaning softly and she rushed to him. He had lost a great quantity of blood from a wound in the shoulder and another in the knee. She removed his coat and tried to dress his wounds as best she could.

She cradled him trying to decide how best to get him home where she could clean him up and have the surgeon look at him. A British officer came along and offered to assist her in getting him to the house. Together they half carried the semiconscious James down into the village and his bed. Thus ended the first major battle in the Peninsula of the War of 1812.

HISTORICAL NOTES: James Secord spent the rest of the war convalescing from his wounds. The ball in his knee was never removed and remained with him the rest of his life.

There is conflicting evidence over what rank James Secord held at the time of Queenston Heights. He is listed alternately as a Captain, a sergeant in the artillery drivers and a private. Hopefuly further research will uncover the true facts.

Brock was buried in the York Bastion of Fort George and Major Thomas Merritt was one of the pallbearers.

CHAPTER EIGHT
THE WINTER OF 1812-13

After the Battle of Queenston Heights Laura Secord spent long hours nursing her husband, who drifted in and out of fever and delirium from the wounds he had received. The Army surgeon had removed the ball from his shoulder but feared taking the ball from his knee as permanent crippling was the probable outcome of the operation. The only thing Laura could do was keep the wound clean and pray that gangrene do not set in. It would be a long time before James would be fit for any kind of labour.

With the defeat of the American Army at Queenston the militiamen were anxious to get the last of their crops off. The British officers were deluged with requests from them for leave to return to their farms. As the spirit of the enemy appeared to have been temporarily broken, permission was usually granted with the warning to be prepared for recall at a moments notice.

The harvest proceeded without incident although it was a poor one due to the late spring and neglect caused by the callout of the militia. William Hamilton Merritt lost most of his crop because of the constant patrolling along the river prior to the Battle at Queenston Heights.

Meanwhile, the Americans were smarting under the embarrassment of Queenston Heights. General Van Rensselaer resigned his command, which was taken over by Brigadier General Alexander Smyth, a regular officer. Smyth was determined to erase the stigma of both Detroit and Queenston before the end of the year. He boasted on November 9th that he intended to invade Canada before the month was out. The proclamation put the British in the Peninsula on their guard. To thwart any attempt at invasion the British began a bombardment of Smyth's headquarters on the 17th of November destroying the magazine and burning some barracks.

General P. B. Porter, commanding the New York State Militia, was eating dinner when a cannon ball crashed through the roof of his home narrowly missing him.

On the 21st the British bombarded Fort Niagara with red-hot shot. The Americans replied in kind and several buildings on both sides of the river were burned. The British fired two thousand rounds in the engagement.

At three o'clock in the morning on November 28th, in a light snowfall, the Americans slipped silently across the river from Black Rock. They were in two groups totaling 400 men in the advance of the main invasion force. One group was to seize and spike the guns in the battery between Fort Erie and Frenchmen's Creek while the other was to destroy the bridge over that creek to delay any reinforcements sent from Chippawa.

The British were waiting, but, despite heavy fire and the loss of several boats, the first group managed to capture and spike the guns. The second group, however, reached their objective only to discover that they had forgotten their axes in the boats. The British soon counterattacked driving them back to the river.

As dawn broke, gray and overcast, Captain Samuel Hatt of the 5th Lincoln Militia stood and watched in amazement as the main American invasion force began to embark in full view of the British defenders. Hatt had led his flank company at Detroit and Queenston and helped drive away the American advance party that was attempting to destroy the bridge at Frenchman's Creek in the early hours of that morning. Despite warnings and threats from their officers more and more men lined the shore to watch the enemy as if it were some entertainment conjured up by the high command.

It was late afternoon before the troops

were fully embarked, some had sat in their boats for hours with snow falling and ice rushing past in the swift current. A boat bearing a flag of truce then crossed the river demanding the surrender of the British Forces. Samuel Hatt obligingly conducted the officer to see Lieutenant-Colonel Cecil Bisshopp, the local commander, who politely declined to accommodate General Smyth. Much to Hatt's amazement, shortly after the boat had returned to the opposite shore, the American troops began to disembark and head back to their camp.

On the following morning more activity was seen on the American side, but the troops quickly dispersed. The next day embarkation began again and Captain Hatt waited with his company. Again the troops disembarked and

the sound of musket shots were to be heard in the British positions coming from the American shore. Deserters later told a hair-raising story of officers breaking their swords, soldiers smashing their muskets in humiliation and frustration at the behavior of their General. Some even fired into his tent and he was forced to move around in fear of his life. The American regulars went into winter quarters and the militia were sent home.

The British breathed a sigh of relief and the locals began to prepare for the spring planting. All hoped that peace would last long enough to accomplish all the chores required to get the crop in.

While the farmers fretted over the prospects of planting and harvesting the following season, the authorities worked diligently to prepare for the summer campaign of 1813. They had to face a number of difficulties if they were to be successful in defending the province. The lack of sufficient British regular troops was compounded by the total lack of enthusiasm by many of the residents of the peninsula for militia service.

To try to remedy the situation they called on prominent people in the community to help convince their neighbours to come forward. One such person was Joseph Willcocks, a member of the Legislative Assembly of Upper Canada, who worked tirelessly to recruit troops for the new Incorporated Militia Regiment that was being raised throughout the province.

Although he had been a bitter enemy of the government, once war was declared he had thrown himself into the British cause. He had persuaded the Six Nations to come into the war on the British side and had even fought as a volunteer in John Norton's contingent of warriors at Queenston.

Joseph Willcocks came to Upper Canada from Ireland about 1800 at the age of twenty-seven. He worked for his distant cousin, the Receiver-General, Peter Russell and then for the Chief Justice, Henry Allcock. Through Allcock's patronage he was named Sheriff of the Home District in 1804. His political views lost him this appointment in 1807 and he settled down in Niagara. He was elected to the legislature in 1807 and represented his riding until 1813. Joseph Willcocks was to become the Benedict Arnold of Canadian History.

CHAPTER NINE

THE CHASE OF THE ROYAL GEORGE

The movement of Armies in the vast wilderness that was Upper New York State and Upper Canada in 1812 was problematic for both sides. Roads were few and rudimentary making troop deployment difficult and supplying them once they were in position a nightmare for the commissary.

By far the easiest and quickest movement was by water using the existing rivers and creeks to get troops and supplies to their destinations. It became apparent early in the war that the side that controlled the lakes had a decisive advantage when it came to distant points in the countryside. Brock's rapid advance to the Detroit frontier and its subsequent capture was made possible by British control of Lake Erie.

President Madison and his cabinet, in discussing their plans for the campaign of 1813, realized that control of Lakes Ontario and Erie was essential to the success of summer operations. To achieve this objective they planned a naval buildup to to sweep the British from the Great Lakes and keep supply lines open.

With ships to be built and manned, the Americans chose Captain Isaac Chauncey, commandant of the New York Shipyards, to oversee the development of a fleet on the lakes. By the end of September 1812, Seamen, labourers and construction materials were pouring into Sackett's Harbor, the main naval base at the eastern end of Lake Ontario.

At the outbreak of the war the American presence on the two lakes consisted of the six gun brig "Adams" on Lake Erie and the sixteen gun brig "Oneida" on Lake Ontario. The "Adams" hauled down her colours at Detroit leaving the Americans with no ships on Lake Erie whatsoever.

The British naval organization on the lakes had been in place since the days of the French and Indian Wars of the mid 1700s. It was revitalized during the American Revolution and prior to the war was used for conducting government business and moving troops from one outpost to the other. The force, however, was not part of the British Navy, but reported to the military authorities at Quebec. It was known as the Provincial Marine.

The Provincial Marine was woefully undermanned and its officers were of indifferent quality. Captain Andrew Gray, acting Deputy Quartermaster General, reported to Sir George Prevost in December 1812 on the state of his naval arm: "The officers of the Marine appear to be destitute of all energy and spirit, and are sunk into contempt in the eyes of all who know them. The want of seamen is so great that the "Royal George" has only 17 men on board who are capable of doing their duty, and the "Moira" only 10 able seamen. On the other hand the efforts of the enemy are such, that nothing can save our Navy from destruction, the moment navigation opens in the spring."

Prevost was well aware of the short comings of the Provincial Marine. His solution to the problem was to get the Royal Navy Involved. He wrote Lord Bathurst, the Colonial Secretary, and Sir John Borlase Warren, whose headquarters at Halifax controlled naval operations from Newfoundland to the West Indies, asking for veteran officers and seamen from the fleet.

His Majesty's Brig, the "Royal George" was completing another leg of her patrol watching for enemy shipping between Wolfe Island and Amherst Island at the eastern end of Lake Ontario. Lieutenant George Smith, the ship's second Lieutenant had the watch along with Midshipman John Ridout, son of the Surveyor General of Upper Canada. They would soon come about and begin the tedious run back across to Big Sandy Bay where the process would repeat itself.

One of the schooners fired a ranging shot, which fell short. The next slapped through the main sail and a hole appeared as if by magic. "Those schooners are mounted with long 32 pounders by the sounds of it, sir," offered Lieutenant Smith. Just then a ball smashed through the port gangway sending a shower of deadly splinters flying like arrows across the deck. Three men went down and were dragged below.

"Set all plain sail, Mr. Smith, and get the stud-

The winds of early November cut through Smith's boat cloak like a knife. Despite his attempts to control it, he shivered with the cold.

As he thought about calling the captain for the change in course a hail from the masthead made him look up, "Deck there, sail on the port bow." His thought of another merchant schooner on its way into Kingston was cut short by the next call from the lookout, "Enemy in sight," the merest pause, "Brig and four schooners, sir, looks like the "Oneida", sir."

The captain ran to the quarterdeck wiping crumbs from his uniform coat, "Beat to quarters, Mr. Smith, clear for action." The crew rushed to comply with the orders, but Smith knew how shorthanded they were. If they stood their ground and fought the enemy there was little doubt as to the outcome.

"Damn," the captain swore, "They have us in a fine trap.' ' He was right; the Americans had the wind gauge and could run down on them at will where they would have to beat up into the wind to come to grips.

sails on her if you can," ordered the captain. ' 'We'll go round Amherst Island and take the North Channel to Kingston; We'll give them a run." Men swarmed aloft and began to shake out the remaining sails, while others prepared the studsails, which attached to the ends of the yards, to give them a little extra speed.

For two days the "Royal George" led her pursuers up the North Channel taking a number of hits from the schooners' big 32 pounders. Fortunately nothing vital was carried away and they managed to beat into Kingston harbour.

The shore batteries kept the Americans at bay. They soon were forced to withdraw to Sackett's Harbor as the navigation season ended until spring. Winter set in leaving the two sides the long cold months to contemplate the coming battles.

CHAPTER TEN
THE OGDENSBURG RAID

With the unsuccessful invasion of the Peninsula in December 1812 war activity along the Niagara all but ceased until spring. The regulars went into winter quarters at Fort George and Fort Erie. The militiamen were released to their homes to prepare for spring planting, which was crucial to their survival. The British forces in the area also would benefit from a good crop come fall.

Although things were quiet on the Niagara front, activities along the St. Lawrence east of Kingston were ongoing even in the dead of winter. The Governor-General, Sir George Prevost, left Quebec on February 13, 1813 for the long, tedious journey to Kingston to review the military situation in Upper Canada.

Sir George Prevost was born at New York in 1767, the eldest son of Major-General Augustin Prevost of the British Army. He entered the army in 1784 and served in the West Indies. In 1801 he was appointed governor of the Island of St. Lucia and the following year became the Governor of Dominica. For his successful defense of that island against the French in 1805, he was created a baronet. He became Lieutenant-Governor of Nova Scotia in 1808 and in 1811 Captain-General and Governor-General of British North America.

Prevost reached Fort Wellington at Prescott on February twentieth. He was immediately cornered by the commander of the Glengarry Light Infantry, a provincial corps of the regular army, and Lieutenant Colonel Thomas Pearson, Inspecting Field officer. They came forward with a proposal to raid the town of Ogdensburg, New York.

The commander of the Glengarry Light Infantry was Lieutenant Colonel George Macdonell. He was a stubborn Scot who was known to everyone as "Red George." He was indignant at the successful raids of Major Benjamin Forsyth, commanding the American forces at Ogdensburg. In the fall of 1812 Forsyth raided Gananoque and on February seventh led some 200 men and in the darkness to occupy Elizabethtown. He freed all the prisoners from the jail except a convicted murderer and also took some fifty prisoners along with a quantity of muskets and various other stores back to Ogdensburg. This rankled Macdonell who thought that Forsyth needed to be taught a lesson.

Prevost, however, was still hoping to avoid a long war and felt that a raid might just stir up the Americans. His policy had been strictly a defensive one and he was reluctant to authorize a move against Ogdensburg. Macdonell argued that the next American incursion might be a major one cutting off communications between Upper and Lower Canada. He even hinted that Sir George might be waylaid by Forsyth at Elizabethtown on his journey to Kingston.

Macdonell's warning worked on Prevost's mind and on his breakfast stop he sent orders back to Prescott that read: "You will not undertake any offensive operations against Ogdensburg without previous communication with Major-General de Rottenburg, unless the imbecile conduct of your enemy should offer you an opportunity for his destruction and that of the shipping, batteries and public stores, which does not admit of delay in availing yourself of it, as I would not have the essential service of the transport of stores to Upper Canada interrupted on any consideration; nor do I think it proper to beget irritation in the mind of the people of the United States by any act that does not bear on the face of it a just retaliation on the military force of that country for wanton and unprovoked injuries." This was at least an approval for a demonstration and on the twenty-seventh of February the Glengarries with the Glengarry Militia started across the ice to Ogdensburg.

Lieutenant Donald McDermid of the 1st flank company of the 1st Regiment of Glengarry Militia marched with the right column headed by Captain John Jenkins of the Glengarry Light Infantry. The wind chased the swirling snow across the ice in a mad race while here and there flakes piled up as if resting from the game. The bitter cold soon numbed exposed skin and searched for any gaps in his clothing that might allow it to attack the rest of his body as well. The footing was extremely hazardous and more than one man went down taking some of his cursing companions with him.

The sight of Ogdensburg put all thought of cold from his mind as he helped form up his company for the demonstration that was to make the Americans think twice before attempting another raid. Rumour had it that "Red George" Macdonell probably ·would disobey Prevost's order and attack the settlement. No sooner had the thought entered his mind then the advance was sounded.

McDermid encouraged his militiamen as they began to advance. The Americans had not opened fire and the anticipation of the volley that must surely come worked on the nerves of everyone. As they approached the first snowdrift near the bank of the river, the fortifications to their front erupted in a cloud of smoke and fire. The man to McDermid's left cried out and dropped into the drift. The column wavered. Captain Jenkins was down on one knee holding his arm. Another volley sent the line reeling back.

The left column led by Colonel Macdonell

pressed forward and gained the deep snow on the river bank. Although he had received a blast of canister in his arm, Jenkins rallied his men and charged the American positions.

McDermid led his men in a wild charge over the bank of the river toward the American positions. He had turned to see that the line was still moving forward when the world exploded around him. The next thing he knew he was lying on his back in the snow. He struggled to get up and that is when the pain struck and he mercifully passed out.

The charge carried the American position and Ogdensburg fell into British hands. The British lost six men killed and Thirty-four wounded including Lieutenant McDermid. They dismantled the fort, burned the barracks and transferred all the stores and provisions to Fort Wellington.

HISTORICAL NOTE: Lieutenant Donald McDermid's name appears on a pension roll for disabled officers dated 26 October 1816.

CHAPTER ELEVEN
THE CAPTURE OF YORK

April 26, 1813 found the little town of York, the capital of Upper Canada, bustling with people of every walk of life making their way, or at least attempting to, along the muddy, rutted streets that the spring thaw had turned into a quagmire. Teamsters cracked their whips and cursed roundly when a wheel dropped into a deep rut bringing them to a jolting halt.

Toward dusk a rider came galloping into town on a lathered horse and rode directly to the government buildings. A farmer on the Scarborough bluffs had seen the American fleet to the east preparing to anchor for the night.

Matthias Saunders, a shipbuilder living in Markham Township was just preparing for dinner when the signal gun in York was heard summoning the militia to the fort. Saunders was a private in Captain John Wilson's battalion company of the 3rd York Militia. He gathered his gear, bid his wife and six children goodbye and headed out to join his regiment.

Eli Playter, a farmer on the Don River and a Lieutenant in the 3rd Yorks also heard the gun. He had just returned from the fort and quickly retraced his steps arriving just after dark. He immediately found where his company was gathering and set sergeants and corporals at various vantage points to send the men to their mustering area as they arrived. He spotted Matthias Saunders and waved him over.

The sun rose on the 27th of April to a fresh easterly breeze, which allowed the Americans to weight anchor and sail toward York. They sailed past the town, rounded Gibraltar Point and anchored off old Fort Rouille. At eight o'clock the American troops embarked in the small boats that each ship was towing and began the long pull to the shore. The battle for York was about to begin.

Matthias Saunders had spent a sleepless night with his company at Fort York. When word arrived that the Americans were about to land west of the Fort Rouille orders began to pour in for this regiment and that regiment to move out. Saunders' company was split up for various duties. Lieutenant Playter, aware that Saunders had a large family to support, put him in the relative safety of the fort serving a twelve pounder gun. His job was to move ammunition from the portable magazine to the gun when it went into action.

The American ships sailed back against the wind and engaged the batteries and Fort York. Saunders rushed back and forth feeding the twelve pounder, which engaged the American fleet as it passed. It was hot work but Matthias knew that it was better than being in the line with musket fire as well as shells to contend with. At least here he was sheltered most of the time.

Reports and rumours came and went as wounded and stragglers came into the fort. The Americans had landed and were slowly pushing forward. A tremendous explosion heard earlier had been the traveling magazine at the Western Battery that accidentally ignited killing thirty-five men. Some said that Major General Sheaffe was going to abandon York and withdraw to Kingston.

In the confusion several militia units, which had not moved from the fort area, were formed up in a hollow next to the garrison. Some managed to get themselves organized but the sight of the battered regulars moving to the rear greatly discouraged them.

Sheaffe had finally made the decision to retire east toward Kingston as all hope of defeating the invaders had long passed. He ordered the regulars to begin the long march east leaving the town to fend for itself.

The general was determined to leave the

Americans nothing of military value and ordered the vessels in the harbour and on the stocks burned and the grand magazine at Fort York destroyed. The latter order, from some oversight, was not passed on to everyone with disastrous results.

Inside Fort York Matthias Saunders fretted over the order to burn the vessels in the stocks at the same time recognizing that it was necessary. Every ship builder grew attached to the vessels they built, especially during construction. To him the ships were not merely wooden ribs and planking but living things each with its own personality and idiosyncrasies.

He sighed as he struggled with the portable magazine, determined to carry it off so that it would not fall into the hands of the enemy. As Saunders made preparations to move his charge to the east, Lieutenant Playter, who had returned to the fort, was picking up his coat and advised the female cook that she had best leave as the Americans would soon be arriving.

He stepped out and noticed Saunders attempting to carry off the portable magazine. He was about to tell him to leave it when the world around him exploded in a shower of stone and timber. Playter had been standing in the shelter of a stout timber wall and the force of the blast, although quite near, missed him and all he had to show for it was a few scratches and a dusty uniform. When his hearing had returned and the dust had settled he looked around at a scene of utter destruction. Bodies lay scattered among the debris that littered the area. Playter moved among the rubble and found Matthias Saunders lying near his magazine with blood pouring from a leg that had been shattered by a large stone. He managed to stop the bleeding and help soon arrived taking Saunders off to the surgeon.

Saunders awoke to find himself stretched out on a table. He couldn't remember how he got there or why. Then the pain hit him and he let out a scream. He finally realized that it was a surgeon looking down at him and shaking his head. Cold fear overtook him, but before he could react someone pinned his arms and legs while another forced neat spirits into his mouth.

The surgeon picked up the long sharp knife from among the saws and other instruments that he had resting in a tub of warm water to lessen the shock of the first cut. Matthias' eyes grew wide as he watched the knife descend toward his leg. They had put a strap between his teeth to keep him from biting his tongue. They were taking off his leg! With the first touch of the knife Matthias mercifully passed out.

York fell that day and the Americans occupied it until May 8th. They burned the Parliament Buildings and other public works as well as looting private property contrary to the terms of surrender. Much bitterness lingered with the citizens of York against General Sheaffe whom they felt had abandoned them to their fate.

HISTORICAL NOTES: Matthias Saunders clung to life for almost a month before dying May 25th.

Eli Playter became a Captain in the 3rd Yorks in 1816 and served in the Legislative Assembly from 1825 to 1828. He died sometime after 1853.

CHAPTER TWELVE
THE BATTLE OF FORT GEORGE

At two in the morning, May 25, 1813 William Hamilton Merritt stood at Vrooman's Point and scanned the far bank of the river. Since the capture of York in April and the subsequent anchoring of the American fleet off Fort Niagara, an invasion was expected at anytime. Merritt and his dragoons had spent the past twelve nights in the saddle patrolling between Niagara and Queenston watching for activity that would signal the beginning of the landing.

After fifteen minutes of carefully examining the river Merritt remounted and led his weary troop toward Fort George, each man watching and listening for any sign of the enemy. The eastern sky was just showing the first glow of dawn as Merritt answered the challenge of the first picket a mile from the fort. Once inside the gate his only thought was of a sparse breakfast and then off to catch a few hours sleep before the cycle would begin again.

Merritt was awakened by the sound of cannon fire and the crashing of shells in the fort. Dressing as he ran, he quickly reported to Brigadier General John Vincent commanding the British forces. His orders were to send out patrols and watch the river and lakeshore for the first sign of an invasion force.

The bombardment became heavy and as Merritt left the general he saw a plume of smoke rising from one of the barracks. The Americans were using heated shot and one had finally lodged in a place where the fire control parties could not get at it to douse the smoldering timbers. Soon the entire building was in flames.

The resumption of the bombardment of Fort George lead General Vincent to draw some of his force to the riverbank away from the lakeshore. To defend Fort George the British had a company of the 49th Regiment under Captain Ormond and a detachment of militia Artillery, one hundred and thirty men in all. From Queenston to the mouth of the Four Mile Creek were thirty gunners of the Royal Artillery with five field pieces under Major William Holcroft, one thousand and fifty regular infantry, three hundred and fifty militia and fifty Indians.

This force was divided into three small brigades. One under Lieutenant Colonel Harvey guarded the river, another under Lieutenant Colonel Myers watched the lakeshore, while the third under Vincent remained in the fort ready to go to the support of either of the other two.

The morning of the 27th awoke to a thick fog with a stillness in the air as if the Peninsula was holding its breath with anticipation. A picket from Captain Robert Runchey's Company of Coloured Men suddenly saw the bow of a ship's boat come looming out of the heavy mist. The alarm was sounded. It was not until the fog lifted, however, that it became clear that the Americans intended to land on the lakefront. Subsequently, the only force immediately available to oppose the landing was Runcey's Company and the Glengarry Light Infantry, who had been dispatched to Two Mile Creek. It was this unit, along with Captain Runcey's company, who met the first wave of enemy troops. They were quickly reinforced by elements of the Newfoundland Regiment and the 1st Lincoln Militia. After a sharp engagement they were forced to fall back on the regulars of the 8th Regiment who moved up in support. Having suffered three hundred and fifty-eight casualties in three hours, Vincent ordered Fort George abandoned and began a slow withdrawal toward Burlington Heights.

Merritt and his dragoons were kept busy harassing the advancing Americans and running orders between the various bodies of troops. On the 28th the army reached DeCew Falls and Merritt led a party from Shipman's Corners (St. Catharines) to link up with the

main army there.

He returned to his father's house on the Twelve Mile Creek the following day remaining there until midnight. Merritt left the homestead in the dead of night and proceeded to Grimsby to take command of the rearguard.

Over the next few days he fought a controlled action, ambushing the enemy wherever possible and making stands at the creek crossings forcing the enemy to deploy into line. He then ordered a quick volley before retiring. This tactic was repeated at every opportunity costing the Americans precious time in forming back up into marching order to continue the pursuit.

Subsequently he retreated to Stoney Creek arriving there on the 1st of June. For the next week Merritt's light dragoons skirmished with the advancing enemy while the main body prepared their defences on Burlington Heights.

Merritt was greatly disturbed by the chain of events that followed the withdrawal from Fort George. He sent a dragoon with orders from Vincent for the force at Chippawa to withdraw through Beaverdams toward Burlington Heights. The militia was sent home and Merritt feared that Vincent intended to abandon Upper Canada altogether.

Many residents of the province had long held the belief that the Americans were certain to win the war and were waiting to switch sides at the first sign of impending victory. The retreat of General Sheaffe toward Kingston and withdrawal of British forces from the peninsula was surely the sign that the Americans would soon control the entire country. Many quietly prepared, not only to welcome the invaders, but to work actively for their success.

Joseph Willcocks followed the retreat from Niagara with a heavy heart. He had seen all this before in his native Ireland, the hopeless fight against superior odds. Worse was the price to be paid for being on the wrong side, the loss of everything. With the fall of Fort George, Willcocks, After much soul searching, decided to offer his services to the Americans as a scout. Joseph Willcocks did not intend to end up on the wrong side this time.

HISTORICAL NOTES: Heated shot used to bombard Fort George was a very delicate operation for the gunners of the American Artillery. Cannon balls were put into a furnace until they became red hot at which time the ammunition handlers would carry them in an iron cradle to the gun. The cartridge of powder was rammed home and then a wad, well soaked with water, was inserted. The glowing ball was then rammed in. Another soaked wad topped off the loading and the gun was fired quickly lest the ball burn through the first wad blowing up the gun. The ball would embed itself into a wooden structure setting it alight unless doused quickly.

Captain Runchey's Company of Coloured Men was made up of escaped slaves who had settled in the Peninsula. Many of their descendants live in the Peninsula today.

CHAPTER THIRTEEN
THE BATTLE OF STONEY CREEK

Captain Merritt watched as the American foraging party moved toward his small patrol of dragoons along the dusty road. One American private struggled with a chicken that seemed determined to return to its former home. Other foragers carried everything from sacks of grain to household furnishings. Bringing up the rear was a sergeant leading a cow. Billy Green, a local farmer who was scouting for Merritt, let out a soft curse as he recognized the cow belonging to one of his neighbours. The neighbour had seven children and it was the milk cow that the Americans had confiscated.

Merritt waited until the enemy was almost up to them before ordering a sharp volley and the charge. The American sergeant managed to raise his musket and fire before being cut down by a sabre, but the fight was a short one and the foraging party was taken prisoner with a few minor wounds with the exception of the sergeant who died in a pool of blood by the road side. One trooper of the dragoons slumped forward in his saddle, wounded by the American sergeant.

For the week following his arrival at Stoney Creek this was the task that Merritt took on, harassing foraging parties and attacking the enemy's flanks as he made slow progress toward Burlington. It was nerve-racking work that kept a constant knot in his stomach as his dragoons ambushed and were ambushed by the enemy.

The Americans finally reached Stoney Creek on June 5th with thirty-four hundred troops made up of infantry, artillery and dragoons. To oppose this force Brigadier General Vincent had eighteen hundred regulars plus Merritt's Provincial Dragoons, and sixty picked men of the Lincoln Militia. Although the odds were not overwhelming by any means, the fate of the British force was in great doubt.

Billy Green had joined Merritt around the fire as the latter ate his dinner. Green was waiting for Lieutenant Colonel John Harvey to go and reconnoitre the American camp. Green told Merritt that the Americans were camped so haphazardly that they might be successfully attacked that night despite the disparity in numbers.

As night was falling Harvey returned to urge Vincent to take the initiative and strike at the Americans. Vincent concurred and plans were hastily prepared.

A half hour before midnight Harvey led seven hundred men from the King's Regiment and the 49th Foot toward the American lines. Merritt, with his Dragoons and a mixed force were held in reserve to follow up any success or cover the withdrawal if things went wrong.

It was a particularly dark night and the troops crept forward using the man to their front as a guide. The leading troops could make out the shadowy form of the first sentry. Everyone stopped as a dark form separated itself from the main body and disappeared into the trees. The dark form reappeared and signaled the advance past the luckless sentry who lay sprawled in the underbrush. Each sentry in turn was dispatched with the bayonet in the same way.

The troops began to form up just beyond the first line of fires in the American lines. Merritt's dragoons moved forward and with a shout all charged the camp firing as they went.

Merritt spurred his horse and he was among the Americans with his sabre slashing and jabbing in a scene of confusion and noise. The Americans, groggy with sleep, were attempting to form some sort of defensive line by the light of their smoldering fires.

Sergeant Alexander Fraser of Major Charles Plenderleath's company of the 49th Foot fired his musket and charged with the

bayonet into the fray. The fighting was close and furious and Fraser found himself face to face with the American general, William Winder, who raised his pistol at the same time as Fraser raised his musket. Fraser informed Winder that if he moved he would die. Winder threw down his pistol and sword and surrendered.

The Americans had at last been able to organize some resistance and the battle raged unabated. Colonel Harvey, fearing that the Americans might see the size of his small force and overwhelm it, ordered the withdrawal from the field.

Brigadier General Vincent in the meantime had become lost in the woods and all feared that he had been captured. Harvey sent Merritt and Billy Green in search of their commander. As dawn broke over the battlefield Vincent came walking back into camp having lost his hat and his horse in the woods.

Command of the American forces had devolved on Colonel James Burns of the 2nd Light Dragoons and immediately he ordered a retreat to Forty Mile Creek. Once again Merritt's dragoons were busy harassing the enemy's rear.

The appearance of the British fleet, under Sir James Yeo, off Forty Mile Creek forced the Americans to continue their retreat toward Fort George. The fleet landed troops and one of them, Sergeant James Commins of the 8th or King's Regiment, wrote to a friend: "It being the King's birthday we gave them a Royal Salute in honour of our old King, but the Yankees did not participate with us as they did not seem to relish our anniversary mirth."

Merritt's dragoons along with a number of Indians chased the Americans all the way to Fort George. On the evening of June 9th the Americans burned Fort Erie and withdrew their forces from Chippawa and Queenston.

This American setback had left Joseph Willcocks in a precarious position. He was now guilty of treason and there was nothing left for him but to join the American cause wholeheartedly. He sought an audience with the American commander and offered to recruit a force of Canadian Volunteers to fight for them.

The Americans held on to Fort George and the Village of Newark where Willcocks endured the sneers of his neighbours. He would not soon forget their arrogance and they would pay for their insolence. He led his volunteers into the countryside raiding and burning the homes of his late constituents.

Merritt was kept busy chasing these irregulars and managed to engage and capture a number of them, but Willcocks always evaded the net. The name Joseph Willcocks became synonymous with traitor among those fighting for their homes throughout Upper Canada.

Victory had slipped through the American's hands once again. The war in the peninsula was to continue through the winter and into the fall of 1814.

CHAPTER FOURTEEN
THE BATTLE OF BEAVERDAMS

After the battle of Stoney Creek Brigadier General Vincent established his main headquarters at Forty Mile Creek. To keep the enemy off balance he also established an advance base at Twenty Mile Creek under Lieutenant Colonel Cecil Bisshopp. Strong pickets were pushed forward to cover the two main roads leading to the Niagara River. One under Major P. V. DeHaren at Twelve Mile Creek watched the road leading to Niagara and Fort George and the other under Lieutenant James Fitzgibbon, quartered at the home of John DeCew, covered the St. Davids-Queenston Road.

Vincent's force now consisted of two companies of the 104th Regiment, the light company of the 8th or King's Regiment, a few Six Nations Indians, 350 Iroquois Indians from Caughnawaga in Lower Canada and the militia including Merritt's Troop of Provincial Dragoons, perhaps one thousand total. Vincent estimated the American force at Fort George to be six thousand strong and he was reluctant to assault his old headquarters.

Merritt's dragoons, in the meantime, continued to skirmish with American foraging parties and raiders led by Willcocks, and another notorious irregular from Buffalo named Cyrenius Chapin. The Indians also gave the Americans fits, slipping up on their pickets sometimes within sight of the fort itself.

The new American commander, Brigadier General John Boyd, was exasperated by the harassment and the humiliation of being cooped up by a much smaller force. He was determined to regain the initiative and subsequently ordered Lieutenant Colonel Charles Boerstler of the 14th U.S. Infantry to march on the 23rd of June and attack the British under Fitzgibbon at DeCew House near Beaverdams.

On June 21st Laura Secord answered an incessant pounding on her door. The sight of three American officers greeted her. One of the three apologized for disturbing the household but they would require a meal from her. They entered without waiting for a reply.

Laura stoked up the fire and went to gather her ingredients while the stove heated up. As they ate the three officers discussed the surprise that was in store for DeCew House on the twenty-third. A young lieutenant wondered out loud if the pickets covering the roads would be sufficient to provide the secrecy they were counting on.

Laura was in a quandary as to what to do. If Fitzgibbon were unaware of the American intention the gains made since Stoney Creek might be wiped out. What could she do with this information she had overheard? James was in no shape to make the journey to warn Fitzgibbon even if he was able to dodge the American pickets who had sealed off the village. Perhaps her brother, Charles Ingersoll, who was an officer in Merritt's Dragoons would know what to do. He was recovering from an illness at the home of his fiance, Elizabeth Secord, at St. Davids and she was determined to get to him. Fortunately she had made a habit of going to see him so perhaps the Americans would let her through.

She left early on the morning of the 22nd and worked her way along the St. Davids Road still not sure if she could get past the American pickets. A sudden challenge brought her up short and an American sergeant demanded her business. Laura explained that she was going to nurse her sick brother at the Widow Secord's mill in St. Davids. Much to her relief he let her pass.

She found Charles too ill to make the journey and the only male in the house was only fourteen and needed at the mill. Elizabeth Secord agreed to accompany Laura in an attempt to find William Hamilton Merritt at Shipman's Corners. The two headed out into

the growing heat of the day.

They soon left the road and cut through the woods to avoid detection. They reached Shipman's but Captain Merritt was not there. Elizabeth, always in frail health, developed sore feet and Laura was forced to leave her there.

Laura headed out again determined to get word to Fitzgibbon about the impending attack. She crossed the bridge on the Twelve Mile Creek and after wading several streams started up the hill toward DeCew House. As she neared the top of the long climb an Indian suddenly jumped out in front of her and demanded to know where she was going. She explained her mission and the Indians escorted her to Fitzgibbon sending scouts ahead to raise the alarm.

Boerstler set out early on the 23rd of June for Queenston and his mission beyond. Besides his own regiment, his force included companies from other infantry regiments plus a troop of light dragoons and a company of light artillery. He marched with seven hundred men under his command. Acting as guide was Cyrenius Chapin.

A prolonged period of rain had turned the roads of the peninsula into a quagmire that slowed the progress of men and wagons to a crawl. The force marched a mere seven miles the first day reaching Queenston in the early evening tired and hungry. They rested where they stopped without building fires for fear of tipping off the British as to their intent.

Starting out early on the morning of the 24th, the American column made slow progress down the St. Davids Road. To avoid the worst of the roads they moved up the mountain to higher ground passing through Stamford on the way to Beaverdams. As they approached their objective they entered a wooded area where the road was merely two slippery wagon tracks. They pushed forward unaware that unseen eyes marked their progress.

Dominique Ducharme, commanding the Iroquois from Lower Canada, had chosen the site well. He placed his own Caughnawaga warriors on the right and the Six Nations under John Brant on the left. As the enemy entered the woods warriors crossed in behind them and those in front opened fire. A running battle resulted in many casualties among the Americans who eventually made a stand in a hollow. They attempted to reverse their march but their wagons became bogged down and the war whoops of the Indians and the casualties unnerved Boerstler.

At this point in the battle Fitzgibbon appeared with a company of British regulars, the only troops available to him. He could not have stopped the American advance even with the punishment they were taking from the Indians. He decided to try a bluff. He demanded the surrender of the American force in the name of his immediate superior, Major DeHaren, who was rushing from Twelve Mile Creek with reinforcements but had not yet arrived.

Boerstler wanted to see the British regulars. Fitzgibbon stalled. Finally DeHaren came on the scene with two companies of the 104th and the light company of the 8th. Boerstler surrendered.

The Battle of Beaverdams or the Beechwoods as it is sometimes called, was an Indian battle and Indian victory in every respect. The British regulars under Fitzgibbon did not fire a single shot. Of the Indians in the battle the Caughnawaga warriors bore the brunt of the fighting suffering casualties of fifteen killed and twenty-five wounded.

Major John Norton of the Six Nations stated after the battle: "The Caughnawagas fought the battle, the Six Nations got the plunder and Fitzgibbon got the credit." The Caughnawagas returned home to Lower Canada in disgust.

Beaverdams gave the British forces in Upper Canada new heart and gave Canada a legend in Laura Secord.

CHAPTER FIFTEEN
THE BATTLE OF LAKE ERIE

Commander Robert Barclay, the one armed senior British naval officer on Lake Erie, inspect his little flotilla with some pride. Although it was undermanned and the quality of the seamen was suspect, he felt they could give a good account of themselves against the Americans.

The corvette "Detroit" was without her proper guns and there was little prospect of them arriving quickly. She was designed to carry sixteen 24 pound carronades and four long 12 pounders. It was decided to split up the ordinance among the ships to arm her. The guns taken from the floating batteries were replaced by guns from Fort Malden.

The task of shifting the guns was not an easy one. The barrel of a long twelve weighed almost two tonnes and its carriage just under half of that. For hours work crews strained with block and tackle to sway the guns aboard ship and to place them.

When all was completed Barclay reviewed the ships under his command. They were: the "Detroit" of three hundred tons mounting seventeen guns and two carronades, of which he took personal command; the "Queen Charlotte" of two hundred tons with three guns and fourteen carronades commanded by Commander Robert Finnis; the "Lady Prevost" of ninety-six tons with three guns and ten carronades, Lieutenant Edward Buchan commanding; the "General Hunter" commanded by George Bignell of seventy-five tons mounting six guns and two carronades; the "Little Belt" of sixty tons with three guns; and the thirty-five tons Chippawa commanded by John Campbell mounting a single nine pounder. In total Barclay could muster six vessels with thirty five guns and twenty-eight carronades. The crews of the squadron totaled four hundred and forty.

Despite the preparations that were made, there were some nagging problems. The guns were fired by means of a flintlock similar to those used on a musket. However, the flintlocks in the Lake Erie squadron were so old and decrepit that the gun captains were forced to trigger their guns by firing a pistol at the vent. This greatly reduced the rate of fire.

The American squadron commanded by Master Commandant Oliver Hazard Perry consisted of the two hundred and sixty tonne "Lawrence" mounting two guns and eighteen carronades commanded by Perry himself; the "Niagara" of two hundred and sixty tons with the same compliment of guns and carronades; the eighty-five tons "Caledonia" with two guns and a single carronade; the "Ariel" of sixty tons mounting four guns; the "Somers" of sixty-five tons mounting one gun and one carronade; the sixty ton "Scorpion" had same armament; the "Porcupine", the "Tigress" and the "Trippe" of fifty tons each with a single gun mounted on swivels rounded out the squadron.

Unlike Barclay more than half of Perry's crews were from the eastern seaboard and many had combat experience., There were even some veterans from the "Constitution" that was refitting at Boston. The Americans boasted nine ships with crews totaling five hundred and thirty-two men.

Barclay waited for his expected reinforcements but when none arrived he gave orders to weigh anchor at 3:00 p.m. on the 9th of September, a Thursday. They sailed away from Amherstburg in search of the Americans.

At dawn the next day a hail from the masthead shook the sleep from everyone's eyes, "Deck there, enemy in sight." Barclay steadied his glass with his good arm and watched the American squadron fighting its way out of its anchorage at Put-in-Bay. One thing was in his favour at least, the wind was blowing lightly from the southwest giving him the weather gauge, that is, his ships would be

between the wind and the enemy.

They were still five kilometres apart at 10 a.m. when the fitful breeze died away. To Barclay's chagrin it immediately returned but this time from the southeast. The enemy now had the weather gauge.

At 11:45 a bugle sounded aboard the "Detroit" and the entire British line broke into songs and cheering. The battle of Lake Erie was about to get underway.

Barclay ordered the gunner to try a ranging shot and one of the "Detroit's" long 24 pounders belched fire and smoke. The round shot fell short. A second shot was seen to strike the Lawrence on the forward bulwark and Barclay could picture the flying splinters raking the deck.

The "Lawrence" began to close with the "Detroit" but the British gunnery was taking a terrible toll. Not only was the "Detroit" hammering away at the "Lawrence" but Master's Mate John Campbell had his "Chippawa" firing his tiny 9 pounder at her as well.

Elsewhere the "Queen Charlotte" was having problems. The "Niagara" and the "Caledonia" were engaging her at a distance and she could not bring all her guns to bear. To compound matters, in the early minutes of the battle a round shot killed Commander Finnis leaving Barclay without his most experienced captain. Lieutenant Thomas Stokoe who took over command also fell with a splinter wound. Command devolved to Provincial Marine Lieutenant Robert Irvine.

By 2:30 p.m. the "Detroit" had reduced

the "Lawrence" to a floating hulk and Perry was seen leaving her. He transferred his flag to the "Niagara", which had escaped serious damage to that point. As soon as Perry was clear, the "Lawrence" struck her colours.

Perry took command of the "Niagara" and bore down on the "Detroit" to engage her with his carronades. Barclay watched the oncoming brig with much apprehension. The "Detroit" was in a bad way and the enemy almost unmarked, then a blast of canister struck him in the back tearing his shoulder blade. Command of the ship fell to his second lieutenant, George Inglis.

The "Niagara" pounded the "Detroit" with her carronades and Inglis ordered the bow of the ship to be brought across the wind bringing the starboard battery into action. A shuttering crash brought cries of alarm from the battle weary crew. The "Detroit" had collided with the "Queen Charlotte" entangling their rigging. The two ships lay wallowing helplessly. The "Niagara" crossed her bow and raked her from stem to stern.

The Niagara broke the British line pounding the British ships from both starboard and larboard batteries. The deck of the "Lady Prevost" was empty except for the tragic figure of her commander, Lieutenant Edward Buchan who was seen hanging over the rail screaming in agony from a terrible wound. Perry saw this and ordered his larboard battery to cease firing.

The "Queen Charlotte" struck her colours as the "Detroit" broke free from their embrace. Inglis tried to get his ship under control but to no avail. Since the ensign had been nailed to the stump of the mast Inglis ordered that a white flag be waved as a sign of surrender. The Battle of Lake Erie was over.

Barclay tendered his sword, but Perry refused it telling all the British officers to keep their weapons as a sign of their gallant fight. Control of Lake Erie now passed to the Americans with grave consequences for the forces at Amherstburg.

CHAPTER SIXTEEN
THE BATTLE OF THE THAMES

The rider galloped into Amherstburg on his lathered mount and went directly to Major General Henry Proctor's headquarters. The news soon spread throughout the little community that the Lake Erie Squadron was no more. Those with loved ones serving in the squadron begged the rider for news of their husbands and sons, but he had no information to share. They were in for a long, agonizing vigil before hearing of the fate of the sailors under Barclay's command.

As British fortunes ebbed and flowed on the Niagara frontier the situation at Detroit had become very precarious. Proctor had enjoyed some initial successes against the Americans, but, the problem of supplies was wearing down his resolve. In addition the arrival of a large American force under William Henry Harrison, a future President of the United States, forced him to pull his troops back to the river at Detroit.

The defeat of the squadron on Lake Erie made the situation even worse. American control of the lake compounded the supply problem immensely.

Proctor was no Brock. No bold plan emerged to reverse the situation. Against the protests of the great Shawnee chief Tecumseh, he planned to abandon the western parts of Upper Canada. To abandon the Detroit frontier was to abandon the western Indians who had fought beside the British since the beginning of the war.

On September 27th Proctor evacuated Detroit and Amherstburg. Thus began the long march up the Thames River toward far off Burlington. The troops were accompanied by a disillusioned Tecumseh with one thousand of his warriors.

Tecumseh was exasperated. He pleaded with Proctor to make a stand at Matthew Dolson's farm and then again at McGregor's Creek, but he would have none of it. The column pushed on mile after mile with the morale of the British troops dropping like the military baggage that fell by the wayside along the route.

The wagons moved slowly despite the rapid pursuit of the enemy. It was soon apparent that Proctor was losing control of his little army. He spent most of his time with his family leaving the day to day command to his subordinate, Lieutenant Colonel Augustus Warburton. The rear guard even failed to destroy the bridges behind them and only the presence of mind of the Indians kept the bridge at McGregor's Creek from falling into enemy hands. Techumseh and his warriors succeeded in tearing down the structure with their bare hands.

The Shawnee warriors just managed to dismantle the bridge at McGregor's Creek when their scout reported American cavalry approaching. Tecumseh placed his men in the woods along the creek bank and waited as the American patrol cautiously moved up to the opposite side. The troopers began to ford the creek. Tecumseh bided his time until the lead rider was three quarters of the way across and most of the troop was in the water. The bushes erupted in a wall of fire sending the men and horses reeling. The Americans plunged up the far bank in full retreat leaving the screams and thrashing of wounded horses and dying men to mark the effectiveness of the warriors volley.

The warriors held their ground for an hour until the main American force came up and formed up for a charge to carry the Indians position. As they waded across the creek the Indians fired a last volley and melted into the woods.

Tecumseh sat by the fire with Oshawana who led the Sioux and Chippewa warriors. Oshawana deferred to the Shawnee chief as the leader of the Indian forces because of the

great respect that all the western tribe had for him. With them was William Caldwell who had been a captain in Butler's Ranger and had settled in Essex County after the American Revolution. He now commanded the Western Rangers sometimes referred to as Caldwell's Rangers. Caldwell chose to fight alongside the Indians, because of a deep respect for Tecumseh.

Tecumseh reasoned that Proctor, whom he considered a coward, would have to stand and fight here, near the Moravian Mission, because of the proximity of the American army to his own. He discussed with his two friends the tactics for the battle that was sure to come.

The following morning the British regulars formed up for battle. It was obvious, even to the casual observer, that the long retreat had taken the fight out of them. They held ground with a swamp on their right and the river on the left, on the surface, at least, an excellent defensive position. Tecumseh immediately directed his warriors and the Rangers into the swamp to affect a flank attack against the Americans as they advanced.

The American cavalry came at the charge and, despite the flanking fire of the Indians, carried the British line. To Tecumseh's amazement the British fired two volleys and surrendered. The chief rallied his force and fought on. His voice could be heard over the gun fire encouraging and leading his warriors.

William Caldwell threw his musket catching a running Kentuckian full in the face. Like most of the Indians he had run out of ammunition and followed their example resorting to the hatchet and knife.

Caldwell spotted Tecumseh leaning on his musket directing some warriors to a critical point in the battle. He seemed determined to wipe out the disgrace of the British surrender.

Tecumseh's eyes met Caldwell's and he moved his arm revealing a gaping wound to his chest. He stumbled slightly and Caldwell signaled two of the chief's warriors who rushed to his side. They carried him deep into the swamp with the rest of the warriors following. The American victory was complete.

As the fighting began Proctor had attempted to rally his troops but soon fled the field leaving the surrender to Warburton. Nothing lay between Harrison and the Niagara Peninsula but open country, however, the season and his extended supply line forced him to turn his army back to Detroit. He then pushed on to Fort George before being called to Sackett's Harbor.

HISTORICAL NOTE: Proctor was court martialled for his conduct in the retreat from the Detroit frontier. He was reprimanded and suspended from rank and pay for six months. Tecumseh died of his wounds and his warriors buried him in a secret grave somewhere in the swamp in which he had fought so bravely.

CHAPTER SEVENTEEN
THE BATTLE OF CHATEAUGUAY

As Harrison was driving Proctor from Amherstburg toward Burlington, two American columns, one under Major General Wade Hampton and the other under Major General James Wilkinson gathered resources for an attack on Montreal. Hampton was to march from Plattsburg, New York to Caughnawaga opposite Lachine. Wilkinson was to march from Sackett's Harbor and make a feint toward Kingston and then rush down the St. Lawrence to link up with Hampton.

Hampton spent the summer of 1813 training his army. In September he deemed them ready and marched from Cumberland Head with four thousand regulars and some New York Militia arriving at the borders of Lower Canada on the twentieth. His advance guard surprised a small picket at Odelltown and proceeded up the Odelltown-L'Acadie Road.

To oppose this force Captain Joseph Saint-Valier Mailloux commanded a few Indians and the Frontier Light Infantry. This unit was formed from the flank companies of the six battalions of embodied militia after the first attempted invasion in 1812.

Mailloux was able to hold the Americans near LaColle until reinforcements arrived from the 4th Battalion of Embodied Militia under Major Joseph-Francois Perrault. After a brief skirmish and a night of Indian war whoops, Hampton retired as far as Chazy, New York. His excuse for the withdrawal was the lack of water for the horses and cattle necessary to sustain his army.

From Chazy Hampton moved west to the upper reaches of the Chateauguay River and established his headquarters at Four Corners just below the Canadian border. He dallied there for twenty-six days before renewing his march to Montreal.

Hampton marched down the Chateauguay with fifty-five hundred infantry, one hundred and eighty cavalry, and an artillery battery consisting of eight 6 pounders, one 12 pounder and a howitzer. Making up this army was the 4th U.S. Infantry and detachments of the 5th, 10th, 29th, 31st, 33rd and 34th U.S. Infantry Regiments; a squadron of the 2nd U.S. Light Dragoons; a detachment of the U.S. Light Artillery Regiment and some New York State Militia.

To meet this invasion the British depended on a force of French Canadian Militia under Lieutenant Colonel Charles M. de Salaberry. He had formed the Provincial Corps of Light Infantry known as the Canadian Voltigeurs at the beginning of the war.

On October 21st Hampton began his advance. He approached the Canadian position on the 26th and found the militia entrenched behind an abatis. After reconnoitring the ground he formulated his plan of attack. He ordered Colonel Robert Purdy to cross the river with fifteen hundred men to take the Canadians from the flank at the ford across the Chateauguay in the rear of the British position. Upon hearing Purdy's men open fire he intended to take the abatis in a frontal assault.

Lieutenant Colonel de Salaberry stood behind the first abatis and waited for the Americans to appear. He had with him three hundred and fifty men made up of the light company of the Canadian Fencibles commanded by Captain George Ferguson, two companies of Voltigeurs commanded by two brothers Jean-Baptiste and Michel-Louis Juchereau-Duchesnay, a company of the 2nd Battalion Sedentary Militia of Beauharnois under Captain Joseph-Marie Longuetin and twenty-two Indians. The reserve consisted of twelve hundred militia and one hundred and fifty Indians all under the command Lieutenant Colonel George MacDonell who had successfully raided Ogdensburg in February 1813.

The pickets were exchanging fire and the main American force was formed up for the attack, but to de Salaberry's dismay and relief they remained in their position. He sent one Voltigeur company to the river bank to fire into the American force he suspected was trying to outflank his position.

At eleven o'clock Purdy's advance companies took a detachment of Sedentary Militia commanded by Jean-Baptiste Brugiere by surprise throwing them back toward the river. The timely arrival of the left flank companies of the Lower Canada Select Embodied Militia under Captains de Tonnanour and Daly steadied them, however, and they held their ground.

Macdonell ordered a sally against Purdy's advance companies driving them back toward the main force. It was attempting to sort itself out after wading through a swamp to reach their objective. Purdy's troops were thrown into complete confusion.

At two o'clock Purdy received orders from Hampton to withdraw four miles upriver, cross over and rejoin the main force. As he moved to obey, Brugiere and Daly attacked Purdy's entire force. With a volley of musketry the militia advanced.

This volley finally drove Hampton into action. He ordered Brigadier General George Izard to form up and advance on the abatis. De Salaberry, thinking to strengthen the morale of his militiamen, raised his pistol and took aim at the advancing Americans. The pistol jumped in his hand and a mounted officer fell from his saddle to the mad cheering of the Militia who sounded bugles up and down the line. A roar of musket fire erupted from the Canadian line.

The advance continued with the Americans delivering disciplined volleys driving in the skirmishers of the Canadian Fencibles. The Americans could smell victory and began to cheer. De Salaberry, sensing a turning point in the battle ordered his men to cheer louder and sounded the advance. MacDonell took up the call and the size of the Canadian force appeared much larger than it actually was. The American line hesitated. Their moment had passed. Their fire slackened and de Salaberry turned his attention to the other side of the river where Daly's and Brugiere's companies were hotly engaged.

Lieutenant Benjamin Schiller of Daly's company kept his men under control as they approached Purdy's main force. His captain was leading the two companies into close proximity with the enemy. He heard the order to kneel and fire. The volley spat out at the American line. The return volley whistled over their heads, but he saw Daly flinch. Although wounded Daly led a bayonet charge on the American line. He quickly went down with another wound and Brugiere fell at the same time. Schiller found himself in command.

They closed with the enemy, but it was soon apparent that they could not carry the day and Schiller ordered the retreat. As he moved back he saw Daly laying in the bush and was determined that he should not be captured. He drew his sword and faced an American officer who came charging through the bush. Their swords clanked together and Schiller could smell his hot breath as he pushed him away. For a few minutes the savage duel continued until the American officer caught his foot on a root. Momentarily off balance, he left himself unprotected. Schiller swung his sword decapitating the American. He scooped up Daly and ran after his men.

De Salaberry stood on a stump and watched as the Americans burst from the woods onto the opposite river bank to be brought up short by volleys of musketry from the Voltigeurs on his side of the river. The Americans reeled back under the combined fire of the Voltigeurs and Schiller's rallied force.

Hampton had had enough. Sounding the retreat the American army withdrew toward their camp and later back to American territory. Three hundred and fifty largely French Canadian Militiamen, with the help of twenty-two native warriors, turned back Five thousand American regulars at the Battle of Chateauguay. This was truly a Canadian victory.

CHAPTER EIGHTEEN
THE BATTLE OF CRYSLERS FARM

While the army commanded by Major General Wade Hampton planned and attempted their invasion of Lower Canada, following the Lake Champlain route, Major General James Wilkinson was preparing to descend on Montreal from Lake Ontario. On paper the chances of success were very impressive with Hampton's five thousand and Wilkinson sitting at Sackett's Harbor with eight thousand troops. However, Wilkinson and Hampton were enemies and the latter resented having to serve under his rival. What should have been a well coordinated plan was, in fact, one party ignoring the other to the detriment of the project.

The secretary of war, John Armstrong, also put in an appearance at Sackett's Harbor disrupting the planning of the campaign. He insisted on an attack against Kingston, while Wilkinson preferred a direct assault on Montreal. When Armstrong finally agreed Wilkinson changed his mind and opted for Kingston and so it went. Montreal was finally agreed on as the primary objective.

Wilkinson left Sackett's Harbour on October 17th at the head of his army in a flotilla of bateaux and headed down the St. Lawrence. Trouble struck almost immediately in the form of an early snow storm. The Americans became snowbound on Grenadier Island with a number of their boats being damaged beyond repair.

Despite the cold Wilkinson pressed on. Part of his army was forced to march down the American side while the remainder took to the boats. On the night of November 6th the boats quietly slipped past the British guns at Fort Wellington.

At Kingston Lieutenant Colonel Joseph Morrison of the 89th Regiment sat with Colonel John Harvey of the 49th going over the latest intelligence. The Americans were stormbound on Grenadier Island apparently headed for Montreal. Morrison had 600 regulars under his command as well as some Canadian Fencibles, a detachment of Canadian Voltigeurs from Lower Canada, a number of Indians and some militia gunners with one 6 pounder gun totaling about 800 all ranks. He also had available a number of gunboats under Commander William Mulcaster R.N.. Although his force was too small to challenge Wilkinson, he felt that they could keep the Americans under observation and harass their rear.

On November 8th The Americans reach the Long Sault Rapids. They deployed a force under Winfield Scott on the Canadian shore to oppose any attempt to interfere with the movement of the bateaux through the rapids. On the 10th Scott's troops along with Jacob Brown's brigade began to march on Cornwall leaving John Boyd's brigade to deal with Morrison's small force. As the American bateaux began to move through the rapids Mulcaster's gunboats opened fire and the small, outnumbered British force attacked.

Lieutenant John Sewell of the 49th Regiment sat shivering and attempting to cook a piece of breakfast bacon on the point of his sword. He had slept on the cold ground in rain and sleet dreaming of that hot piece of pork that now dangled over the fire. His dream was shattered, however, by the call to assembly.

Sewell popped the warm bacon in his mouth, pulled on his gray overcoat and joined his company. They were to advance and attack the enemy. Sewell moved just ahead of his men confident that his sergeant was keeping the ranks in perfect order. He had often thought it strange that a man going into battle, perhaps to die, could worry about how straight the line was.

They moved up behind a heavy rail fence and halted. Looking over the field of winter wheat to his front, he knew that no better place

could be found to face the Americans. Open fields where the British regulars could fight a European style battle with precision drill movements. Yes, if they had to face a numerically superior force this was the place to do it. This was the type of warfare that the 89th and 49th understood.

A sudden volley to the front caught Sewell's attention. The French Canadian Voltigeurs had caught the advancing Americans in the open had driven them back. A renewed attack, however, drove the Voltigeur back and to the left of the 49th's position. As Sewell watched the entire 89th Regiment wheeled from its position facing east to one facing north and delivered precise volleys that force the Americans to break and run.

The brigade to the 49th's immediate front

began to advance and Sewell watched his men as the command to form echelon by platoon was sounded. Having completed this parade ground drill movement, he controlled his platoon as they poured rolling volleys of musket fire into the advancing enemy.

The order to advance came and Major Charles Plenderleath led the 49th against the American guns 120 yards to their front. With grapeshot whistling around his ears Sewell advanced, helping his men tear down two snake fences that were impeding their progress. His captain, in the middle of issuing him some instructions above the roar of battle, pitched backward into the mud and lay still. Sewell plunged on leading the company toward its objective.

A new danger suddenly sprang up to

Sewell's right. A troop of American Dragoons was thundering down the King's Highway toward their position. If they could get behind them they could charge their rear turning the tide of battle against them. Sewell only half heard Captain Ellis' orders to his company on the right flank, "halt...front...pivot...cover...left wheel into line...fire by platoons from the centre to the flanks."

Ellis had wheeled his company backward to the left to face the cavalry. Ellis waited as the cavalry charged down on his company. Sewell looked over to make sure he was still standing. He was about to call over to see if something was amiss when smoke and fire erupted from the British line shattering the American charge and eliminated the threat. Ellis had held his fire until the last minute to maximize the effect. His company wheeled back to the advance and the 49th carried the enemy guns.

The Americans were forced to withdraw from the field and that night recrossed the river to the American side. The army pushed on to make their junction with Hampton's army beyond the Long Sault, but Hampton, having been defeated at Chateauguay, refused to meet Wilkinson at St. Regis. Wilkinson, ill and discouraged, abandoned the campaign. The British and Canadian forces had won a great victory against overwhelming odds.

Lieutenant Colonel Morrison's troops had outfought the Americans that day, however, one American unit caught his attention. He was so impressed by the U.S. 25th Infantry's steadiness in battle that he sent a note to its commander, Colonel Edmund Gaines, hoping that they might meet after the war as friends.

On the Niagara Frontier the humiliating defeats of Stoney Creek and Beaverdams forced the Americans to withdraw into the confines of Fort George. The victory at the Thames did little to lift the morale of those garrisoning the Peninsula. Foraging parties were ambushed and Merritt's Dragoons harassed pickets and patrols alike. The pickets especially were vulnerable to Indian attacks that kept them constantly in a state of agitation.

The scene was set for one of the most callous acts of the war. An act that would have far reaching consequences for Americans living on the east bank of the Niagara.

CHAPTER NINETEEN
THE BURNING OF NEWARK

Despite the British successes at Chateauguay and Crysler's Farm, which ended the threat to Montreal and Quebec, the British defeat at the Battle of the Thames left Niagara in a delicate state. To relieve the pressure on his meager resources Sir George Prevost ordered the evacuation of all of Upper Canada west of Kingston. Fortunately Major General John Vincent, who had resumed command in that theatre of operations, felt a withdrawal to Burlington would suffice.

The Americans were quick to take advantage of the withdrawal from the Peninsula and reoccupied Queenston and Chippawa. Joseph Willcocks and his Canadian Volunteers also wasted little time in exacting a price from the loyalists left behind. The farms of those who had once been neighbours and friends were pillaged and burned. Willcocks arrested prominent loyalists and had them sent to prisons in the States. Among them were Thomas Merritt, William Hamilton's father and eighty year old Peter McMicking of Stamford who had been High Constable of Lincoln County, a coroner and a town warden. Merritt was so incensed by the treatment of his father that he wrote in his journal of, "having taken many a long and weary ride, in the lonely hours of the night, in hope of catching Willcocks and making an example of him and all traitors."

Upon hearing of the arrests and raids Colonel John Murray convinced Vincent that a small force should be moved back into the Peninsula to protect the inhabitants. Subsequently Murray led a force of three hundred and seventy-eight regulars of the 8th Regiment and some volunteers, including Merritt's Dragoons, to Forty Mile Creek establishing a base there.

Captain William Hamilton Merritt cautiously led his troop east away from their base at Forty Mile Creek. Where were the Americans?

The Indians had been in contact with their pickets the previous evening, but now they were nowhere to be found.

A signal from an advance scout brought Merritt forward at the gallop and the tail end of the American column was sighted tramping toward Twenty Mile Creek. Merritt sent his dragoons charging down the road scattering the American infantry and fighting a sharp engagement with some American cavalry who quickly withdrew from the scene. Some of the infantry tried to resist, but many quickly surrendered and were marched off as prisoners of war.

With the American Army in retreat Murray pushed his force forward to Twenty Mile Creek and then to Twelve Mile Creek. The Americans, meanwhile, had pulled back to Fort George. Their commander, Brigadier General George McClure, was in a precarious position. The enlistment of many of his troops was expiring and his force began melting away. Willcocks' raids had further alienated the local population and when one of Murray's outposts soundly defeated a probing force sent out by McClure, he decided to withdraw to Fort Niagara.

December 10th dawned cold and blustery with snow drifting in the lee of the well kept picket fences. Joseph Willcocks had been beside himself when told of the plans to abandon the Peninsula. He had at least wrung the order to burn the town from McClure on the pretext of denying shelter to the advancing British troops. Willcocks was determined to punish his former neighbours for slights, real and imaginary, that he had suffered since going over to the Americans. The Canadian Volunteers and American militiamen went door to door warning the inhabitants to get out what they could. At dusk the destruction began.

Willcocks mounted the steps of the Dickson house, fire brand in hand, followed by

two of his men. The younger of the two had explained that the woman was ill in bed and couldn't get up. Willcocks ordered the two to carry her out, bed and all, and lay her in the snow. He had arrested William Dickson and had him sent off as a prisoner to the United States and was determined to destroy whatever property he could. The two lads wrapped her in blankets as best they could and put her in a snow drift while Willcocks fired the house and its contents. He walked away leaving Mrs. Dickson in the snow to watch her home burn to the ground.

Weeping women and children looked on as their world was turned into a pile of ashes. Their immediate concern was shelter. There were four hundred refugees who would die of exposure if cover could not be found quickly.

Captain Merritt reported to Colonel Murray. The glow in the eastern sky could only mean one thing and with Merritt's dragoons they rode off to investigate.

The troop approached Fort George from the south and cautiously reconnoitred the area. The Americans were pulling out and the only troops remaining were the rear guard, which consisted of some of the Canadian Volunteers. Merritt signaled the charge routing the enemy, killing two and taking a number of prisoners.

The scene that greeted them in the town was beyond belief. Every building except one was a pile of glowing embers and the streets were littered with furniture that some had been able to save before their homes were torched. People were desperately seeking shelter.

Some moved toward the fort and Butler's Barracks, which had been spared for some inexplicable reason, others built crude shelters against chimneys using half burnt boards as roofing while still others began the bone-chilling trek to farms in the neighbourhood.

Dawn brought the misery of the town to full bloom. Many a snowdrift yielded up the frozen bodies of women and children who could not find their way in the bitter cold darkness of that December night in 1813.

The mood of the British troops was dark indeed. Every man from Colonel Murray to the lowliest private had one thing on his mind; vengeance!

HISTORICAL NOTE: General McClure was relieved of his command and dismissed from the army for his part in the burning of Newark.

CHAPTER TWENTY
THE CAPTURE OF FORT NIAGARA

The burning of Niagara produced a sense of rage among even the battle hardened British regulars. The Canadian militia seethed at the sight of their families and neighbours living in squalid conditions, some under canvas in the dead of winter.

McClure's argument that it was necessary to deprive the British of shelter proved rather weak when Butler's Barracks, with its store of tents and other military equipment was spared. McClure's remark that, "the enemy is much exasperated" was an understatement indeed. The call for retribution was universal.

On 13 December events moved forward that would see the rage unleashed on the American frontier. On that day Sir Gordon Drummond was appointed president of the council and administrator of Upper Canada. He also assumed command of all the troops in the province.

Drummond was born in Canada while his father was serving in the Quebec garrison. At age eighteen he entered the army and served in Egypt, Holland and the West Indies. He rose rapidly through the ranks and held the rank of Lieutenant General upon his arrival in the land of his birth.

Drummond wasted little time. He arrived at Vincent's headquarters at St. Davids on the seventeenth and ordered an immediate attack on Fort Niagara. Colonel John Murray was put in command to lead a surprise night attack. To accomplish this Captain Merritt's Dragoons scoured the country for boats. Members of the Lincoln militia manhandled some craft overland from Burlington Bay. To Merritt's disappointment exhaustion and a case of the grippe precluded him from participating in the raid.

Late on the night of 18 December Murray embarked his troops at a ravine some two miles up stream from their objective. The force consisted of detachments of the 100th Regiment of Foot, the Royal Scots and the flank companies of the 41st Regiment of Foot. The Lincoln Militia acted as boat handlers and guides.

Private Shadrack Byfield of the 41st Foot stood in the narrow ravine waiting to enter the boats for the slip down river to Fort Niagara. His attempt to restore some feeling in his feet by stamping them brought a whispered order to keep quiet from Lieutenant Bullock. To the sergeant he added his inevitable, "take that man's name." Not only was Byfield cold, but now, if he survived, he could expect extra duties or drill.

The boats, with muffled oars, worked their way down river and landed near Youngstown. As Byfield formed up with his company he saw Sergeant Andrew Spearman of the Grenadier company of the 100th Foot slip by. It would be hard to miss the huge bulk of Spearman. For all his size it was said that he moved like a cat. He surprised the lone picket outside a tavern and choked him into silence. After forcing the pass word from him he dispatched him with a single thrust of his bayonet. The rest of the picket inside met the same fate.

As Shadrack marched by the open tavern door he could see the sprawled bodies lying carelessly about the floor and he grimaced. However, he knew that the element of surprise, so essential to the operation, had to be maintained. They would likely face an aroused garrison when they assaulted the main gate otherwise.

As they approached the main gate Byfield heaved a sigh of relief. All was quiet. His company was to follow up on the main attack by the 100th. His feet and the cold were forgotten as a sudden challenge from the main gate broke the silence.

Sergeant Spearman had walked across

the drawbridge and gave the sentry the password in answer to his challenge. As the luckless guard opened the sally port Spearman strangled him with his massive hands.

A shout of alarm came from inside the fort as the gate swung open. Byfield charged through and formed up with the rest of his company in reserve. Nothing had been left to chance. Even in the darkness he could see Daniel Servos, an officer in the Lincoln Militia standing with a piece of wood to jam in the gate to keep it from being closed behind them.

There was an eerie feeling of fantasy about the battle that ensued. Except for a volley from the Royal Scots, who were holding the salient angle of the fort, little musket fire was in evidence. The fort was taken at the point of the bayonet and in the stillness of the night the cries of the wounded seemed to be magnified.

Sixty-five Americans were killed and sixteen wounded with the British sustaining casualties of six dead and five wounded. Also captured were twenty-nine guns, seven thousand muskets, seven thousand pairs of shoes and a huge stock of clothing originally captured by the Americans from the British.

One of the prize trophies of the victory was the American battle flag that flew from the flag pole during daylight hours. Byfield knew that it would be sent to England as a spoil of war.

The cells at the fort yielded up eight Canadians who had been arrested by Joseph Willcocks, among them eighty year old Peter McMicking of Stamford. Those same cells were quickly filled with some of the four hundred prisoners taken.

Shadrack Byfield stood warming himself by the fireplace in the comfortable stone house in Youngstown. He had marched out to take up picket duty with the rest of his company. His sergeant gave each man fifteen minutes in the commandeered house to thaw out from the bitter cold. Looking around, he could feel some pity for the owners. Tomorrow it probably would be a pile of ashes.

With the dawn of 19 December reinforcements arrived under Major General Phineas Riall. He gave the order to burn Youngstown and the Tuscarora village before marching on to Lewiston. The Americans on Lewiston Heights decamped as the British approached leaving behind some guns and two hundred barrels of flour. After torching Lewiston Riall pushed on to Manchester and Fort Schlosser. Since the bridge at Tonawanda Creek had been destroyed by the retreating enemy, the general turned back to Lewiston crossing over from there to Queenston leaving the American frontier in flames.

As a tribute to the work of Merritt's Dragoons for their fine work in the planning stages, Murray allowed them to a share in the prize money. The booty captured was valued at a million pounds. Each private soldier received two pounds sterling as his share. Shadrack Byfield was a rich man by barracks standards.

In the meantime General Drummond was putting plans in motion to end the threat to the peninsula for the balance of the winter. His next objective was the destruction of the forces at Buffalo and the town itself.

HISTORICAL NOTE: The place of embarkation for the troops that stormed Fort Niagara is marked by a plaque at McFarland House on the Niagara River Parkway. The ravine used by men like Shadrack Byfield on that night is still there today. The flag captured in the battle was presented to the Prince Regent who eventually returned it to Sir Gordon Drummond. This flag was recently returned to Fort Niagara by Cherry Drummond, the Baroness Strange, a descendant of Gordon Drummond.

CHAPTER TWENTY-ONE
THE BURNING OF BUFFALO

The capture of Fort Niagara and the retreat south along the river was a sad time for Joseph Willcocks and the Canadian Volunteers serving in the American army. Benajah Mallory, Willcock's second in command and a former member of the Legislative Assembly, fought a rearguard action with sixty men. Their determination only delayed the inevitable.

Meanwhile Shadrack Byfield's company was advancing on Fort Schlosser. Just short of their objective they captured a blockhouse taking eight prisoners. Byfield was one of the men detailed to guard them. As they marched their prisoners toward Schlosser the sound of footsteps behind them gave them a moment of concern. Byfield volunteered to go back and investigate. He seized the officer of the guard from the blockhouse who had escaped in the confusion. The captured officer complained that someone had stolen his boots at which Shadrack reached into his pack and offered the man his extra pair along with a tot of rum that he had been saving. The young officer burst into tears. It seemed that he had not expected to be treated with such kindness.

The officer had further reason to weep when he reached Fort Schlosser. On entering the fort he spied the body of a fellow officer sprawled out on the floor. It was his best friend.

The burning of Niagara was avenged. The entire frontier from Youngstown to Tonawanda Creek was a smoking ruin.

The plans for the followup raid to the capture of Fort Niagara was put into motion quickly. On the 28 December the orders were issued and every man made aware of the contents. To accomplish this the 8th Regiment, the light company of the 89th, a few men from the 41st under the designated second in command, Major Richard Freud, and some militia and Indians moved down to Fort Erie. Their objective was to capture any stores that could be moved and destroy the rest including two armed schooners and a sloop wintering at Buffalo. The towns of Buffalo and Black Rock and any other dwellings that might shelter the enemy were to be burned to the ground.

Lieutenant-General Sir Gordon Drummond was a man of action and a strict disciplinarian. He wished to avoid the ransacking of American property that had been the trademark of the American occupation of the Peninsula. His orders for the raid on Black Rock and Buffalo prescribed death as the punishment for troops caught looting.

Shadrack Byfield sat in the boat trying not to interfere with the militiamen who were rowing. He discovered, from a conversation with one of them while they waited to embark, that they were from the 3rd Lincoln Militia. Most were farmers from the immediate district and enthusiastic about the coming raid. Many were disappointed at not being included in the attacking force as they had lost crops and homes to marauding American irregulars and the Canadian Volunteers under Willcocks. When Byfield had settled into his place one of the militiamen had whispered, "Throw a torch for me, lad."

The approach to a hostile shore was always nerve racking for Byfield. It was almost better to cross under fire. The waiting for the challenge and the volley of fire to come out of the gloomy darkness was unbearable. Suddenly the oars were tossed and the troops began to land in the cold of a December night. Byfield stomped his feet in an attempt to restore circulation. He was sure that he would never be warm again.

The invaders crossed the captured bridge over Scajaquada Creek taken by the light infantry at the point of the bayonet. Byfield noticed a solitary corpse lying spread eagle in the snow and mused that at least one man's

lack of vigilance had cost him dearly. Murmured orders brought him and his fellow privates into defensive positions on the far side.

Dawn was greeted by the sound of cannon fire to the south where the American gunners were opposing the second landing above Black Rock. The order to advance came and they moved off behind a skirmish line of Indians. Everywhere the American militia fell back before the advancing British who quickly reach the outskirts of Buffalo.

Byfield's company filed into Buffalo and as they passed up Main Street near Seneca he witnessed a disturbing scene. Through the window of a house he saw an Indian attempting to take down some curtains and a woman struggling to stop him. The woman suddenly struck the Indian with a butcher knife at which he raised his hatchet and the woman disappeared from sight. At that moment the first whiffs of smoke began to drift down from Seneca Street and soon the whole area was in flames.

A British squad commanded by a lieutenant set fire to the house where Byfield had seen the grisly scene. The widow St. John, a neighbour, managed to get the body of the woman, Sally Lovejoy, out of the house and extinguished the flames. That night, with help, they moved her back into her house laying her on the rope cords of an old bedstead.

The destruction of the frontier took days to accomplish and a haze of smoke blanketed the area as if to hide the agony of the settlements. The widow St. John's cottage was spared by Riall who left a soldier to guard it. However, the big house, which she had turned into a hotel was prime for the torch. The British fired it, but Mrs. St. John and her daughters managed to extinguish the flames.

The respite for the St. John's was short lived. A British patrol set the big house on fire again. When the widow protested that this was her livelihood the officer in charge pointed out that she had a roof over her head, which was more than the Americans had left Canadian widows at Niagara. The house went up in flames along with that of Sally Lovejoy. Her house became her funeral pyre.

With the destruction of Buffalo the settlers of the peninsula could sleep peacefully without fear of a sudden raid from the American side. For the time being the campaign of the summer of 1814 was still frozen in the winter snow.

CHAPTER TWENTY-TWO
THE WINTER OF 1813-14

The destruction of the American side of the Niagara ended the threat of raids on the struggling inhabitants of the Peninsula for the winter of 1813-14. Despite this reprieve much damage had already been done to the villages and farms of the area. An all too familiar sight was the family salvaging what they could from their burned out home, loading up a wagon and moving to winter quarters. If they were lucky they had friends or relatives to assist them, otherwise a bleak winter under canvas was what a few had to look forward to. Many sought refuge at York and made the torturous journey around Lake Ontario to the capital.

The citizens of Niagara began the monumental task of rebuilding the charred ruins of their community. The satisfaction of the retribution visited upon their American neighbours lost its glow in the misery and hardship of their own circumstances. Working under impossible conditions they contended with shortages of every kind; lumber, nails, and tools.

While the inhabitants of the Peninsula struggled to survive the men in power began planning for the coming campaign. On Lake Ontario and Lake Champlain a major naval buildup was in progress. The largest ships ever to appear on the great lakes were under construction at places like Sackett's Harbor, Kingston and York. 1814 would be the critical year in this war.

Changes at the high levels of command were made in Upper Canada. Lieutenant General Gordon Drummond became President of the Legislative Assembly and Administrator of Upper Canada. He had acted as Sir George Prevost second in command since 1811 and knew what was needed to win. The legislative assembly was called into session in February to make the tough choices necessary. With the burning of the government buildings in April, 1813 the assembly met at Jordan's Hotel and Tavern, which now doubled as the government chamber.

Drummond was a Canadian born officer, the first to command the army. His opening speech, although gracious, left no doubt as to who was in charge. He continued the ban on the distilling of grain to ensure that every grain of wheat, oats and barley went to feed the starving population. He was also concerned about the high number of American sympathizers in the province. The jail in the provincial capital was bursting with prisoners accused of treason and other offences of disloyalty.

Given the situation Drummond demanded extraordinary powers, among them: the suspension of the right of habeas corpus in some cases, the right to confiscate the property of convicted traitors and the right to declare martial law when necessary. The legislature granted him the first two that he requested, but denied him the last. Drummond was not to be thwarted. Without this power he would have been unable to commandeer provisions for the troops in the field. Despite the risk of censure he convened his executive council, which he completely dominated, to give him the power to declare martial law.

Money was another problem faced by Drummond in planning the spring campaign. Debts piled up by Brock on his march to Detroit were still outstanding and settlers were reluctant to sell their produce to the government. To further complicate matters, Canadians disliked paper money. They demanded gold in payment, which was almost impossible to get. Two reasons can be given for the settlers refusal to take paper. One was the real chance of an American victory, which might leave the paper worthless, plus the fact that the Americans had flooded the province with counterfeit bills to undermine the economy.

The troops, as well, were in a bad way. Their discontent stemmed from the lack of pay,

some of which was six months in arrears. Colonel Robert Young, commander of the garrison at Fort Niagara, complained of the number of desertions from the post. To compound matters many of the garrison were ill prompting the medical officer to recommend they be withdrawn.

The Americans were also having their organizational difficulties. Wilkinson's troops, who were wintering at French Mills, were ordered to Sackett's Harbor. From there they immediately began to march toward the Niagara Frontier only to be turned back. The American commander Jacob Brown had misunderstood his orders from Washington much to the grumbling of the troops who were forced to march in the cold. They finally settled down at Sackett's Harbor to await the spring.

The Americans were not the only ones contemplating a march. Drummond devised a bold stroke against the American fleet wintering at Put-in-Bay on Lake Erie. The plan called for the seizure of Amherstburg with a force of seventeen hundred men, and attack the fleet across the ice, destroying it. However, an unexpected February thaw made the ice to soft to attempt it and the whole plan had to be abandoned.

All was not gloomy, however. The grain crop of 1813 had been a good one despite the wet spring. A bumper crop was harvested, especially in Lower Canada. Ironically American beef still poured into the country. De Rottenburg reported that, "Our beef contractor in Albany is back in business and American cattle will soon be moving over the frontier again." Cattle ostensibly gathered for American troops at the Salmon River were driven to Prescott for British use. Thomas Ridout wrote his father that the contractor was a "Yankee magistrate."

In western Upper Canada the inhabitants were at the mercy of American marauders. In February a traitor named Andrew Westbrook led a force on a cattle stealing venture up the Thames. A detachment consisting of the light company of the Royals and some Canadian Dragoons sent them packing but not before they took a number of prisoners including Francois Baby, a prominent local loyalist.

Not all efforts were being made on the military front. In July, 1813 Czar Alexander I of Russia offered to mediate the dispute between the United States and Britain. With Napoleon on the run in Europe the Americans were anxious to conclude a peace before the might of Wellington's army became available for service in North America. However, the trio of John Quincy Adams, Son of the former President of the United States, James Bayard and Albert Gallatin were left cooling their heels for six months waiting for word as to whether the British would accept the Czar as mediator.

In April Henry Clay, Speaker of the House of Representatives arrived in Sweden to head the American delegation. With no British negotiators in sight he summoned Adams and his colleagues to meet him to discuss the situation.

Things took a turn for the worst for the Americans in March when the Allies in Europe captured Paris and Napoleon abdicated his throne. The fear of an overwhelming British force available for Canada had become a reality. Despite this the British finally agreed to sit down and talk. Negotiations began at Ghent in Belgium on May 15, 1814. Many more men were to die before peace was concluded.

CHAPTER TWENTY-THREE
THE ANCASTER ASSIZES

The situation in Upper Canada was precarious in the spring of 1814. The loyalty of many of the inhabitants was in doubt and seemed to swing with the fortunes of battle. To stiffen the backbone of the militia and make the price of treason very clear to the population in general, Drummond prorogued the legislature and ordered the trials of those held in jail for treason be held immediately. There were nine persons ready for trial and another twenty to be indicted.

Twenty-three year old John Beverly Robinson, veteran of Queenston Heights and acting Attorney General of Upper Canada, prosecuted the cases. Robinson's predecessor, D'Arcy Boulton, had been captured while on his way to England and was in a French jail. He had seen the previous Attorney General and aide to Isaac Brock, John MacDonell, killed at Queenston Heights along with his General.

Robinson was a rising star in the circles of the Upper Canada aristocracy. Bishop John Strachan spotted something in him at an early age and took him under his wing. Strachan paid his tuition at his school in Cornwall, took him into his home and generally saw to his well being. He owed his present position to the influence of Strachan.

Robinson drew up abstracts against thirty Canadian citizens for high treason. They had participated in raids with the Canadian volunteers under Joseph Willcocks' second in command Benajah Mallory the previous November and were captured by the Oxford and Norfolk Militia at Port Dover and Chatham.

It was decided to try them in the civil courts for, as Robinson pointed out to Drummond, "Executions of traitors by military power would have comparatively little influence. The majority of the people would consider them arbitrary acts of punishment."

Most of the accused were from the London District and it was felt that the trials should take place as close to their homes as possible. The nearest available site that was firmly under British control was the area around Burlington Heights. Ancaster was chosen and the Union Hotel became the temporary court room. As an example to all, twenty-one farmers stood before a jury of their peers to be judged.

By modern standards one would question whether the jury was impartial. Many of the prospective jurors had voluntarily helped capture the accused. Their farms had been raided and looted by Willcocks' raiders. Robinson commented at the time, "Men who risqued(sic) their lives in the apprehension of these traitors will be well satisfied to have them punished as they deserve."

The trials proceeded and Robinson, determined to give the accused every opportunity to defend themselves, resisted the pressure for summary justice. The pressure came from several sources not the least of which was Drummond himself. He urged Robinson to speed things up so as to give the fickle public an example of what traitors could expect before the coming summer campaign.

Of the twenty-one persons accused fifteen were found guilty and two had to be remanded until the fall as evidence had arrived too late for that session. The guilty stood in the prisoners dock while the judge read out the sentence in the form that had been used for centuries: "That each of you are to be taken to the place from whence you came and from thence you are to be drawn on hurdles to the place of execution, whence you are to be hanged by the neck, but not until you are dead, for you must be cut down while alive and your entrails taken out and burned before your faces, your head then to be cut off and your bodies divided into four quarters and

your heads and quarters to be at the king's disposal. And may God have mercy on your souls."

This is perhaps the one part of all this that bothered both Robinson and Drummond. The Chief Justice, Thomas Scott, quickly assured Drummond that the sentence was never exactly carried out. The executioner usually didn't cut the prisoner down until he was dead.

Robinson now had the job of reviewing the cases and making his recommendations to Drummond as regarded clemency. They were not all clear cut cases. He decided that eight sentences should be carried out, but there were extenuating circumstances in the other cases.

Samuel and Stephen Hartwell had returned to their native United States at the outbreak of hostilities and were captured at Detroit as prisoners of war. Although they were technically traitors they had declared their allegiance from the outset unlike some others who had tried to straddle the fence. As Robinson pointed out to Drummond, "from the former relations between the two countries many cases of such nice discrimination may arise. . . .perhaps from political motives even, it is best not to strain the law to its utmost rigors."

There was also the case of Jacob Overholzer of Fort Erie. Although not the brightest man in the community, he owned a large amount of property. An American who had only been in the province a short time, he became the target of some Canadians of unsavory character who took the opportunity of war to settle some old grudges. They stole his horses and household goods and threatened to burn him out after the burning of Niagara. When Overholzer complained to the authorities the thieves accused him of being a traitor and charges were brought. The magistrate dismissed them as being unfounded, but they were dredged up again and his defence was rejected. Ninety-six of his neighbours drew up a petition asking for a pardon for this honest old man whom they described as being peaceable, sober, hard working and a good neighbour.

Robinson left the issue of clemency up to Drummond, but urged that only the ringleaders of the traitors be executed, perhaps one from each of the London and Niagara Districts. Chief Justice Scott concurred pointing out that, "since example is the chief end of punishment . . . the punishment of a few would have an equal, and I even think a more salutary effect in this province, than the punishment of many."

Drummond decided that the eight listed by Robinson should die and on 20 July 1814 the sentences were carried out on Burlington Heights. The men were made to stand on the tailgates of some wagons and they were driven off leaving them to strangle. Their contortions were such that a cross brace fell striking one of the men on the head killing him. All eight heads were chopped off and put on public display.

Of those whose sentences were commuted one escaped, three were banished from Canada for life and three including Jacob Overholzer died of typhus while confined to the military prison at Kingston three months after the war ended.

Thus ended what was to become known, perhaps unfairly, as the bloody assizes. Drummond had gotten his example and the bloody campaign of 1814 was about to begin.

CHAPTER TWENTY-FOUR
THE SUMMER CAMPAIGN OF 1814: THE PRELUDE

With the coming of spring in 1814 both sides in the War of 1812 prepared for the coming campaign. The Americans faced a crisis as the ice disappeared from the lakes and rivers of the war zone. Napoleon had been defeated in Europe and the British would soon be able to deploy the cream of Wellington's army in the North American theatre. Would Wellington himself come to command the British Army? Regardless of the answer President Madison and his cabinet realized that the summer campaign of 1814 was probably their last chance to make gains before the peace negotiations got underway at Ghent in Belgium.

The Americans had every reason to be optimistic. The Officers who had so badly managed the campaigns of 1812 and 1813 were gone, replaced by younger, fresher minds. The commander of the Left Division of the U.S. Army, which encompassed the Niagara Frontier was Major General Jacob Jennings Brown. At the outbreak of war in 1812 Brown was a militia officer who commanded the St. Lawrence defences. He held off a British attempt to seize Ogdensburg and was instrumental in the defence of Sackett's Harbor in May of 1813.

Brown made the transition from the militia to the regular forces and accredited himself well as a brigadier general in the disastrous St. Lawrence campaign of 1813. He gained promotion, at age thirty-nine to major general in the spring of 1814 and given command of the Left Division.

Brown was fortunate in the appointment of the junior officers in his division. Commanding his first brigade was the twenty-eight year old Winfield Scott. Scott began the war as a captain and quickly rose through the ranks. He was captured at Queenston in 1812 commanding the forces that surrendered to Sheaffe's relief column. This young brigadier general took command of his brigade determined that they would be ready to face anything the British could muster against them.

Thirty-two year old Brigadier General Eleazer Wheelock Ripley commanded the second brigade. Ripley was commissioned a lieutenant colonel in the 21st U.S. Infantry in 1812 and proved an able commander.

The third brigade was made up of militia from New York and Pennsylvania, Willcocks' Canadian Volunteers and the American's Indian allies. Brigadier General Peter Buell Porter of Black Rock commanded this brigade. Porter was a partner in the Porter, Barton Company that ran the portage on the American side of the Niagara. He was one of the few warhawks on the Niagara Frontier.

Brown received orders from John Armstrong, the Secretary of War, giving him the prime objectives of the summer campaign. Brown was ordered to make an attack on Kingston feinting an attack on the Niagara Frontier to mask his intentions. To further facilitate the plan Armstrong sent another letter to Brown suggesting that the Peninsula be his main objective. Armstrong's idea was that this letter should fall into British hands giving his invasion at Kingston a greater chance of success.

Such intrigues were beyond Brown's understanding however, and he immediately marched his army to Buffalo setting up camp at Flint Hill on the shores of Lake Erie. They no sooner settled in then Brown was called back to Sackett's Harbor. He left Scott in command giving orders that the division should be made ready for the coming campaign.

Scott set about the task with a will. He was meticulous in the living conditions of the men. Proper sanitation and fresh food was demanded at all times. The men were ordered

to bath weekly under the supervision of an officer. Cases of disease and sickness dropped almost immediately with the resultant rise in morale. He drilled the division by brigade, regiment and companies for seven to ten hours a day. The Left Division would be ready when the call came.

Meanwhile the British Right Division waited for the Americans to make their move. The division was commanded by thirty-nine year old Major General Phineas Riall. Unlike his American counterpart Riall was a career soldier who had entered the army in 1794. Unfortunately he had seen limited active service in his long career, a flaw that was to haunt him in the campaign to come.

Several circumstances gave the enemy a decided advantage over Riall's forces. While the Americans concentrated their army at Buffalo Riall was forced to scatter his over a wide area. Detachments of the division were stationed at York, Burlington Bay, Fort George, Fort Niagara, Fort Erie and along the entire extent of the Niagara. Indeed he had requested permission from Drummond to withdraw from the Peninsula and concentrate his forces at Burlington. Drummond refused citing the American penchant for harassing the local inhabitants in the absence of British troops.

On the eve of the American invasion the British had twenty-seven hundred troops in the peninsula. The 100th Regiment of Foot was at Fort Niagara and the 1st Foot (Royal Scots) was at Fort George. Detachments of infantry were dispersed along the length of the river with concentrations at Fort Erie, Chippawa and

Queenston. The 8th Foot was in York, but scheduled to return to Niagara in early July. Supplementing this regular infantry force was the 1st and 2nd Regiments of Lincoln Militia, a detachment of Royal Artillery and militia artillery and Major Robert Lisle's 19th Light Dragoons, the only squadron of British regular cavalry in North America.

Also attached to the right division was a large force of native warriors. These warriors came from two groups commanded by two different men. The western nations, refugees from Proctor's retreat from Amherstburg, came from a number of different tribes. The main tribes represented were the Ottawas, Chippewas, Delawares and Munseys. There were also some Wyandots, Fox, Shawnee, Moravians, Cherokee, Kickapoo and Sioux in the group as well. These warriors came under the Indian Department commanded by Lieutenant Colonel William Claus.

The other faction was from the Six Nations of the Grand River under Major John Norton, a Scot who had been adopted by the Mohawks and had become one of their chiefs. There was a keen rivalry between the two groups of natives in the British service.

On 2 July 1814 Brown, accompanied by Scott, Porter and his senior engineering offi-cers scouted the Canadian shoreline and settled on a plan of action. Scott's brigade was to cross the Niagara from Black Rock landing near the ferry dock north of Fort Erie. Part of Ripley's brigade was to cross with Scott while the remainder landed on the opposite side of the fort near Snake Hill. Heavy artillery would be used to pound the British defenders into submission. At evening roll call the orders were read out to the division. The campaign of 1814 was about to begin.

As Winfield Scott's 1st Brigade reached their embarkation area at Black Rock just after midnight on 3 July 1814 the rain began to fall. By the time they began to cross the Niagara at 2 A.M. the rain was falling in sheets.

Scott led in the first boat, which came under fire as they approached the shore. A picket of the 100th Foot, stationed there for just such an eventuality, had spotted the invasion force through the driving rain. It was here that Scott almost became the first casualty of the campaign. Never one to shy away from a fight, Scott tested the water with his sword and, judging it to be only a foot or two deep, plunged in and immediately sank up to his neck. He was hauled back into the boat with all but his ardor dampened.

CHAPTER TWENTY-FIVE
THE BATTLE OF CHIPPAWA

Major Thomas Buck of the 8th Foot, commander of Fort Erie, watched as the day dawned sunny and bright. He had sent off his detachment of the 19th Light Dragoons at the first encounter with the picket to warn Riall that the Americans were landing in force. He now watched as the mass of blue and grey clad Americans manoeuvred before his post. He had only one hundred and thirty-seven officers and men to defend against the might of the American invasion. At 5 P.M. Buck surrendered rather than see his men slaughtered for no good purpose.

Captain William Hamilton Merritt of the Troop of Provincial Light Dragoons sat down with his family to enjoy a celebration. A rare leave had coincided with his twenty-first birthday and Hamilton intended to enjoy this one visage of normalcy in the mayhem of war. Thomas Merritt, his father, was proud of his young son who ably commanded the dragoons in patrolling and harassing the enemy.

A sudden commotion outside brought everyone to the front porch where one of Merritt's men on a lathered horse dismounted on the fly. Saluting awkwardly, he rushed up to his commander and breathlessly told him that the Americans had landed. Merritt met his father's gaze and without a word went to saddle his favorite horse, Hyder Ally. In a few minutes he was galloping for Fort George as fast as Hyder Ally could carry him.

Through the day and night of 3 July the Americans consolidated their position before advancing toward Chippawa. As they prepared for their march a British reconnaissance force under the command of Lieutenant Colonel Thomas Pearson appeared. Pearson had with him two flank companies of the 100th Foot and a contingent of native warriors under the Mohawk chief Major John Norton. Pearson realized that he could not hope to engage the Americans with his small force so he posted pickets on the River Road and withdrew to Chippawa.

British forces were dug in on the north bank of the Chippawa. Five companies of the 1st Foot (Royal Scots), the 100th Foot, the 19th Light Dragoons and Captain James Mackonochie's field brigade of artillery held the position. The 8th Foot (King's Regiment) was on its way from York and was expected early on 5 July. The 1st and 2nd Regiments of Lincoln Militia were also on their way.

To allow sufficient time to gather reinforcements Colonel Pearson volunteered to take troops toward Fort Erie to fight a delaying action. Early on the morning of the 4th he moved forward with the two flank companies of the 100th Foot, the light company of the 1st Foot, a detachment of the 19th Light Dragoons and two 24-pdr. guns commanded by Lieutenant Richard Armstrong RA. As Scott's brigade advanced Pearson deployed his small force behind Frenchmen's Creek after tearing up the bridge planking forcing Scott to deploy his brigade into line. The British fired a round from one of their 24-pdrs. and added a volley musket fire for good measure before retreating down the River Road. It took precious time for the Americans to reform into column and repair the bridge. Pearson repeated this tactic all the way to Chippawa.

As the American column approached the Chippawa the British guns opened fire. In a renewed downpour of rain Scott turned his troops back to Street's Creek where he intended to camp for the night. About midnight General Brown marched into the camp with Ripley's 2nd Brigade and the artillery. With rain beating down on them the exhausted men laid down in the open and slept.

Toward morning the rain stopped and Major David Secord of the 2nd Lincoln Militia sat by the fire smoking his pipe and discussing

the possible plan of action for the day with Captain John Rowe. The fifty-five year old Secord was second in command of the 2nd Lincoln Militia and Rowe commanded one of its flank companies. Both were veterans of the American Revolutionary War and had served in Butler's Rangers. They settled in the Peninsula in the 1780s.

Part of the regiment was to work with the Indians to reconnoitre the American camp just after sun up. The sight of so many of the enemy in the act of getting up was too much for some of the native warriors and they began sniping at the Americans as they went about their early morning duties. This sniping continued throughout the morning.

The British camp became a beehive of activity about noon as the army prepared to

march. *Major Secord talked quietly with John Rowe as Lieutenant-Colonel Thomas Dickson inspected the regiment that was to march with the light companies that day. The two old warriors agreed to compare notes after the action and went to their respective places in the line.* The order came. The troops began to march across the bridge into the meadow from which many would not return.

Meanwhile, in the woods to the right of the line the militia and Indians were engaged in a vicious running fight with Peter Porter's Brigade. Brown had sent them out to flush the British skirmishers driving them away from Street's Creek.

David Secord was formed up with his regiment to face the coming battle. He could hear the war whoops and musket fire drawing near to their position. Pearson ordered the Lincolns forward with the Western Indians and suddenly the Indians and militia who had been sniping at the American camp came bursting through the line followed closely by Porter's troops. Soon the air was alive with the sounds of battle. Here and there men dropped as volleys of musket fire poured in from the Americans. *Secord turned in time to see his friend John Rowe go down.*

Colonel Dickson Suddenly toppled from his horse with a wound in the chest. Fortunately his glasses deflected the ball or it would have been fatal. The rate of fire of the Lincolns began to slacken. Major Secord took command and rallied the men to a greater effort. Despite the pounding they were taking they held their ground and obeyed his orders when the urge to run must have been overwhelming. Porter's men finally broke and the running battle reversed course and the Canadian militia and Indians were doing the chasing.

Meanwhile Riall marched his regulars onto the plain. One of the most significant battles in the history of the regular U.S. Army was about to unfold.

The battle in Samuel Street's wood continued unabated. Lieutenant Christopher Buchner now commanded John Rowe's company, but it had suffered heavily in the fighting. Stephen Peer, a recent immigrant from the United States, was one of those killed. His wife gave birth to their second child, a son, on the twenty-ninth of July at their home on the Portage Road. James Forsyth, whose tavern was a few miles to the north on the Portage Road, left a widow and several children to mourn him.

Despite the casualties the 2nd Lincolns fought on beside Colonel Pearson's light companies of British regulars and the native warriors. Led by David Secord, a merchant from St. Davids, the Lincolns distinguished themselves that day.

While the battle for the woods continued Riall ordered his regulars to advance through a strip of woods onto the plain facing the American camp. The 19th Light Dragoons led Lieutenant Richard Armstrong's artillery battery down the River Road. Within four hundred yards of the Street's Creek bridge Armstrong unlimbered his two 24 pdrs and his 5.5 inch howitzer. Behind them came the three battalions of regulars. They turned west onto the plain and formed line with the 100th Foot on the left flank then the 1st Foot with the 8th Foot on the right. There was not enough room for the three battalions to form a continuous line and the 8th formed a reserve on the right rear of the position.

The American commander, Brown, was out reconnoitring the plain when the British came into view. He immediately sent one of his aides to order Scott's 1st Brigade forward. Scott, who disliked the militia intently, was miffed at having to support them. He did not believe that the British were out in force. However, since he was about to drill his brigade anyway he decided that the plain on the north side of Street's Creek was as good a place as any. Scott's doubts were about to disappear.

The troopers of the 19th sat their horses behind Armstrong's guns. The drums were silent and, except for the scattered musket fire and war whoops from the woods, a stillness settled over the plain as if it was holding its breath. The troopers steadied their mounts as the 24 pdrs spat their defiance as Scott's troops approached the bridge. It was 4:15 P.M.

Scott's brigade crossed the bridge under a steady rain of artillery. His well disciplined troops stepped over their fallen comrades and wheeled into Samuel Street's field of oats at a farm lane to face the equally well disciplined British. The American artillery under Captain Nathan Towson replied to Armstrong's challenge and the general engagement was on.

Riall watched the grey clad American brigade forming up and assumed them to be militia. American regulars were normally dressed in blue. Ironically the British Navy was responsible for Riall's mistake. Their

blockade of the American ports had led to a shortage of blue dye. Riall was confident that the American "militia" would break before the onslaught of British bayonets.

Riall ordered the advance of the 100th and the 1st directing the 8th to counter a move by the U.S. 25th Infantry to outflank the British line. In the centre of each marched the colour party. The line advanced at seventy-five paces per minute stopping frequently to maintain their dressing on the colours. Their commanders, Lieutenant Colonel John Gordon of the 1st Foot and Lieutenant Colonel George Hay, the Marquis of Tweeddale, who had taken command of the 100th only hours before, rode at the head of their battalions. In silence they advanced. It was 4:30 P.M.

When the British line reached a point one hundred and fifty to two hundred feet from the American position the air was shattered by the first American volley. Towson's battery joined in with canister and the British line halted. Gordon and Tweeddale gave the order to fire and the battlefield was soon shrouded in thick smoke. It was 4:45 P.M.

The American artillery cut swaths through the British ranks, but the sergeants closed the gaps as the casualties were dragged away. Despite the carnage in the ranks the British stood their ground and exchanged volley for volley with the enemy.

After twenty-five minutes the situation became desperate for the 1st and 100th and their commanders decided that the only way out was to close the Americans with the bayonet. All efforts to get the battalions moving, however, failed. The concentrated fire of the American infantry and artillery was too much even for the disciplined British regulars. Gordon of the 1st Foot took a musket ball in the mouth and was led to the rear.

Riall, desperate to rally his troops rode recklessly out in front urging the troops forward, but to no avail. Unable to advance and unwilling to retreat the red line continued to take casualties as the fire fight went on.

Finally the flanks of the British line began to give ground and the centre followed suit. Riall saw that nothing would be accomplished that day and ordered the retreat. The two regiments withdrew out of musket range, formed in column of march and moved toward the Chippawa. Their withdrawal was covered by the 19th Dragoons and the 8th Foot. It was 5:10 P.M.

David Secord pulled back the 2nd Lincolns with the light companies and native warriors. Norton, with his contingent from the Grand River heard the retreat sounded. They arrived at the bridge across the Chippawa only to find it already torn down. Fortunately the beams were still in place and his agile warriors were able to cross.

The Americans demonstrated in front of the Chippawa until 6:30 P.M. and then withdrew to their camp. The battle was over.

On the morning of 6 July an officer under a flag of truce went into the American camp with a request, "for the bodies of the officers killed, particularly for the militia; as it would be a great satisfaction for the relatives of the deceased to have them properly interred." The request was refused. Brown was reported to have said, "that he was able to bury all the dead he could kill."

David Secord thought of his friend John Rowe buried somewhere on the battlefield as he completed the list of those killed from his regiment. It was difficult to ascertain how many casualties there were. Some reported seeing a man go down, no, another would say, he was taken prisoner and so it went.

The shock of the defeat weighed heavily on the troops. This was the first time that American regulars had defeated British regulars in a European style battle. Somehow things would never be the same in this war. The stage was set for the bloodiest battle of the war.

HISTORICAL NOTE: The list of the 2nd Lincolns killed at Chippawa is as follows: Captain John Rowe, Captain George Turney, Lieutenant Christopher McDonald, Sergeant John Hutt, Privates Samuel Adams, Joseph Bastido, Lewis Blanshet, Thomas Bloomfield, James Forsyth, John Hill, Alexander McDonald, Stephen Peer, Timothy Skinner, Robert Taylor, John Thompson, and Jacob Wilkinson. (There are variant spellings for some of the above names.) Major General Riall praised the conduct of the 2nd Lincolns in a dispatch published in the London Gazette of August 9, 1814, "The conduct of the officers and men of this Regiment has also been highly praiseworthy."

CHAPTER TWENTY-SIX
THE BURNING OF ST. DAVIDS

Brown and Riall faced each other across the river for three days after the Battle of Chippawa. Brown could not hope to dislodge the British from their position without decimating his army. Riall on the other hand was not strong enough to assault the Americans without inviting total disaster.

On the 7th of July a local farmer, perhaps hoping to save his farm from destruction, told Brown of an old disused logging road that led to the junction of Lyons Creek and the Chippawa. Brown dispatched half of his force on the 8th of July with engineers to bridge the Chippawa. He launched a mock attack in front of Riall's main position to keep him occupied.

The Americans began to build their bridge under fire when Riall, fearing that he would be cut off from Fort George, ordered the retreat down the Portage Road toward Queenston. The Americans followed in hot pursuit. They expected Riall to make a stand on the heights, but on arriving there they found the British gone. Riall had retired to Fort George. Once again it seemed that the Americans had the peninsula in their grasp.

At this juncture the thing that had plagued the Americans from the beginning struck again, lack of cooperation. The American naval commander on Lake Ontario, Isaac Chauncey, was supposed to arrive off the mouth of the Niagara to support the assault on Fort George and Fort Niagara. General Brown arrived in Queenston on July 10th and had a fine view of the Lake from the heights. Where was Chauncey? Chauncey had guns and extra troops needed by Brown. On July 13th he sent an urgent appeal to his naval counterpart to come quickly. Chauncey, however, was laid up with a fever and would not entrust command of his fleet to anyone else. Brown waited in vain at Queenston for the sight of sails on the lake.

Riall was not content to let the Americans rest in their camp. He sent out Merritt's dragoons with the militia and Indians to harass the enemy.

William Hamilton Merritt stood by his favourite horse, Hyber Ally, stroking his neck. Merritt was stiff with fatigue for he had been patrolling and skirmishing with the enemy almost non stop since the withdrawal to Fort George. Things were brightening up, however, as reinforcements arrived daily to augment Riall's army. The 89th, the 103rd and the 104th Regiments as well as the Glengarries and units of the York Militia swelled the ranks of those already there.

On 12 July Riall withdrew his main force to Twenty Mile Creek leaving strong garrisons at Forts George and Niagara. The Americans, unable to assault the forts without the fleet, fell back on their favourite pastime of 1813, looting. They descended on the farms of the district running off cattle and pigs. Willcocks and his Canadian Volunteers were especially troublesome, plundering every house they could find, even stealing soap. The locals had become so incensed by the wanton destruction that they had taken to sniping at the Americans from concealed positions in the woods.

The old farmer reached the edge of the woods just as the American foraging party was leading away his horse. He could see his wife weeping in the doorway of their house. He was too old for militia service, but lately he had taken to carrying his ancient musket with him when he left the farm. He held down his rage as he loaded and took careful aim from the concealment of the thicket. He took a deep breath, expelled half of it and put steady pressure on the trigger. The old gun spat fire and smoke momentarily blinding him. When the smoke cleared he nodded with satisfaction, the man leading his horse lay sprawled on the

completely under his power, were quietly defying him. He nodded to one of his officers and they began their work.

Merritt led his patrol out into the countryside in an attempt to intercept American foraging parties. A troop of American dragoons suddenly came into view and wheeled around, making a dash for their own lines. Merritt led his men in pursuit. Merritt, charging after the enemy, became aware that his sergeant was yelling his name. He reluctantly reined in to see what the trouble was. The sergeant pointed toward the southwest where a huge pillar of smoke surged into the sky.

It could only be St. Davids. They were burning St. Davids. A sense of sadness turned to rage as Merritt watched the column of smoke grow bigger with each passing minute. They were burning the whole village. Merritt turned his troop toward the rising cloud of smoke and galloped hard to reach it. What he found was the burning ruins of forty homes and businesses. It could only be Willcocks he thought, but for once Willcocks was not the culprit. The name Isaac Stone would go down in infamy for this day's work.

HISTORICAL NOTE: General Brown was so enraged by the action of the burning of the village of St.Davids that he dismissed Colonel Isaac Stone from his command.

ground and the horse was running for home. The old man slipped into the woods with musket balls whining harmlessly over his head.

Lieutenant Colonel Isaac Stone of the New York State Militia listened to the report of the young officer of the continuing sniping from the local population and the mounting casualties that resulted. It was to the point that the men's morale was suffering and they were reluctant to forage. Stone decided that these snipers needed to be taught a lesson. He formed up his troops and marched on the loyalist village of St. Davids. Colonel Stone would put an end to the harassment.

Stone stood in the centre of the road that passed through the village of St. Davids. The women, old men and children watched him in silence. He studied their faces. Some showed fear, but most had a look that he could not quite read; he raised one eyebrow in surprise. It was defiance. These people, who were

CHAPTER TWENTY-SEVEN

THE BATTLE OF LUNDY'S LANE

With the burning of St. Davids Canadian militiamen flocked to the British colours while Brown waited in vain for Chauncey's squadron. Each day that the horizon remained empty Brown's position became more precarious. He was dependent on supplies from Buffalo, which were landed at Samuel Street's wharf south of Chippawa. Transport was scarce and his supply trains were constantly harassed on their trip along the Portage Road. On 23 July a letter from Sackett's Harbor realized his worst fears. The navy was not coming.

While Brown fumed at this turn of events British reinforcements poured into the peninsula. The 89th Foot added fresh troops to the campaign while the American strength was reduced to twenty-eight hundred effective soldiers. The heat and disease was taking their toll on Brown's troops.

Riall, with a new sense of optimism, ordered troops to be moved across to the east bank of the Niagara to threaten the American supply line. Brown decided, on 24 July, to withdraw to Chippawa and resupply his army. He next proposed to bypass Fort George and move on to Burlington Heights. A victory there would trap the garrisons at Forts George and Niagara and open the road to Kingston. The ever eager Winfield Scott pressed for an immediate thrust to Burlington that night. Perhaps they would avenge the humiliation of Stoney Creek, but Brown allowed discretion to rule and the army evacuated Queenston and completed the march to Chippawa.

Twenty-five July 1814 dawned bright and sunny promising a sweltering day. At 8 o'clock in the morning Riall set the army in motion and Merritt led his dragoons to scout ahead. They reached Lundy's Lane at noon. About 3:00 p.m. Merritt and several officers rode forward to reconnoitre the ground toward Chippawa for some sign of the enemy.

Meanwhile at Chippawa Jacob Brown fretted over the British intentions. He was convinced that Riall intended his main thrust to be on the east bank and the capture American supplies at Fort Schlosser. One of Brown's weaknesses was his refusal to change his mind once made up. The officer of the day, Colonel Henry Leavenworth, reported seeing British infantry and a troop of dragoons on the Portage Road near the falls. He argued that this was Riall's advance guard for Riall would not expose such a force without heavy backup.

At 5:00 p.m. Brown, convinced that the British were crossing from Queenston to Lewiston, ordered Scott to march toward Queenston to force the British withdrawal back across the river. Scott marched with his brigade plus Towson's battery of artillery and a squadron of dragoons.

Wilson's Tavern, one of the few buildings not destroyed by the Americans, served as a refreshment stop for officers of both sides during that summer of 1814. Merritt and his fellow officers made their customary visit to the widow's establishment that afternoon. Hamilton took in the view of the thundering cataract. The falls had always fascinated him and he never tired of watching the tumbling waters or listening to the constant roar. They were interrupted by an advance scout sent forward by Merritt to watch the road. He came up at the gallop and announced that the enemy was on the move.

Merritt sent the rider on to warn the main body and turned to see Winfield Scott's Brigade march into view. He held Hyber Ally in check and watched the Americans through his glass, attempting to ascertain their number. A puff of smoke and the whine of a musket ball close by his head told him that the enemy was within range. Ignoring the dust kicked up by the firing of the enemy, Merritt coolly saluted

the Americans and rode north toward Lundy's Lane.

The American advance guard burst into the tavern in search of stragglers to be met by the Widow Wilson.

"Oh sirs," she said, "if you had only come a little sooner you would have caught them all."

Scott himself questioned the widow and to save her establishment and aid the British cause at the same time, she told Scott that there were eight hundred British regulars, three hundred militia and Indians with two pieces of artillery with Riall at the junction of the Portage Road and Lundy's Lane. Scott decided to push forward without waiting for the rest of the army, a decision that was to

have a far reaching affect on the outcome of the day's action.

Merritt rode up the hill with the little red meeting house at the summit and reported to General Riall. He estimated a brigade was on the move toward them. Riall told him to await orders.

While he waited he had an opportunity to view the potential battlefield. To the south was the farm yard of Lydia Peer whose husband lay buried at Chippawa. The little farmstead was surrounded by fruit orchards. Some four hundred yards from where he was standing the thick woods began to hem in the Portage Road. To the east of the Portage Road stood another stand of heavy timber. On the hill itself stood the meeting house with an accompanying graveyard. To the east, toward the river, the woods continued to dominate the scene. To the north the hill dropped away and he could see the Portage Road winding its way through the forest toward Queenston. The road running back toward the west went through Decew Falls and reinforcements could be expected from that direction.

Merritt felt that this would make an excellent defensive position should the Americans attack. He was roused from his musings by a rather harassed aide who gave him his new orders. Merritt went to gather his dragoons in preparation for the battle he knew was coming.

Scott moved cautiously up the Portage Road. The thick woods were ideal for an ambush and he had his cavalry scour the trees for signs of British skirmishers.

As Merritt mounted Hyber Ally musket fire announced the steady approach of the enemy as they slowly drove in the outlying pickets. The bloodiest battle of the war was about to begin.

As Scott approached the junction of the Portage Road and Lundy's Lane, Riall, prodded by his new respect for American troops after his defeat at Chippawa, agonized over his next move. He finally sent word to Drummond and ordered a withdrawal back to Queenston.

William Hamilton Merritt stood with the rear guard as Pearson's Light Brigade began their withdrawal. General Riall, fearing an attack in force, ordered the move to form a junction with the main body that was coming up from Queenston. Merritt's orders were to help delay the enemy for as long as possible and then execute a fighting retreat along the Portage Road. Drummond, who was moving up from Queenston, met Riall's column and immediately countermanded the order sending the troops back to Lundy's Lane.

Ensign John Campbell of the Incorporated Militia marched beside his company as they made their way along the Portage Road. It seemed that the promised battle was to be postponed for another day. He wondered if they would be stopping to cook a meal as it was early evening and he had eaten nothing since breakfast.

Suddenly the column came to a halt and the troops ordered off the road. Campbell could see General Riall in conversation with the Commander in Chief, General Gordon Drummond, who was gesturing with his sword toward the south and the enemy. Orders filtered down the line to reverse direction and reoccupy the heights at Lundy's Lane.

A messenger rode to the Twelve Mile Creek to order up the troops camped there. These troops, commanded by Colonel Hercules Scott, consisted of seven companies of the 1st Foot, five companies of the 8th Foot, seven companies of the 103rd Foot, which was Scott's own regiment, two flank companies of the 104th Foot and a detachment of artillery with three 6-pdr. brass guns. Scott also had under his command Lieutenant Colonel Christopher Hamilton's Militia Brigade, which consisted of detachments of the 1st and 2nd Norfolk Militia, 1st Essex, 1st Middlesex, and the Western Rangers. All told Hercules Scott had fifteen hundred regular infantry and two hundred and fifty militia. Scott was quick to get his command in motion.

Meanwhile at the lane Drummond deployed his troops. His best, the 89th Foot, occupied the centre with the right held by three companies of the 1st Foot. The light companies of the 41st held the left with the light company of the 8th and the Incorporated Militia holding the woods to the east.

The rest of the militia took up positions to the west of the regulars. There was elements of the 1st, 2nd, 4th and 5th Lincolns as well as the 2nd York Militia here. The 2nd Lincolns, still mourning their dead from Chippawa, found themselves defending their homes again. Lieutenant Christopher Buchner stood with his son John a short distance from their home, which was situated to the west of the little cemetery near the lane to the Skinner properties. In Buchner's company was Charles and Henry Green whose father, Charles, had donated the land occupied by the meeting house

and cemetery. His home was a few hundred yards from the lane. Sergeant James Lundy, whose father gave his name to the lane, also stood in the ranks. William Biggar, who farmed further out the lane, thought of his wife and children at the Lundy house less than a mile from where he stood. Noah and Gideon Skinner fretted for their farm just a mile south of Lundy's Lane along with John Bender whose father owned much of the property between the Portage Road and the river. They watched as the enemy knocked down their fences and trampled their crops.

Winfield Scott, acting on the intelligence that half the British army was on the American side of the river, ordered his brigade to form up and advance. On clearing the chestnut grove he realized the error of the reports. He knew he was facing the bulk of the British army.

The British guns opened fire and turned the pastoral farm lands to their front into a killing field. The American line stood with only a company of the Twenty-Second Infantry breaking after being hard hit by artillery. The three regiments, the Twenty-Second, the Eleventh and the Ninth fired volley after volley at the British position on the hill, but they were too far away to cause any damage. They, however, were being cut to pieces by the British guns.

Only Jesup's Twenty-fifth Infantry came to grips. Taking a flanking movement through the woods to the east, they caught the Incorporated Militia in the act of taking up a new position. Jesup fired a volley and pressed home his attack. Lieutenant Colonel William Robinson went down with a ball through the forehead, which exited behind his ear. The militia broke and the Twenty-fifth took a number of prisoners.

In the gathering dusk Captain Merritt

escorted two six pounder guns to the crest of the hill and watched as the American guns unlimbered near the farm on the Portage Road. As he rode back toward the rear a volley of musketry made him pull up. Some American infantry had made their way through the woods and had attacked the Incorporated Militia as it switched places with the King's Regiment on the left flank. He could see that several staff officers, including General Riall, who appeared to be wounded, were surrounded by the enemy.

A harried officer ordered Merritt to inform Drummond that he intended to charge the enemy in order to recover the general and not to fire on his troops by mistake. Merritt turned Hyber Ally and spurred him the crest of the hill.

Returning from his mission, Merritt was suddenly surrounded by six Americans and hauled from his horse. They immediately pushed him toward the south along the Portage road. They came under heavy fire from the hill and Merritt almost escaped with another prisoner. The latter got away but Merritt was not as fortunate.

Ensign John Campbell willed himself to remain calm. Colonel Robinson was wounded and being carried to the rear. The enemy had captured General Riall and most of his staff and were gathering on the road. He listened as an officer gave the orders, "Front rank, make ready!" The men cocked and primed their muskets.

"Present!" They raised their muskets to their shoulder taking aim.

"Fire!" The air erupted in fire and smoke. As the smoke cleared Campbell could see the enemy trying to form up. Another volley tore into their midst and several men fell withering on the ground. The cries of the wounded could be heard above the roar of guns and the bark of the muskets. The Americans attempted to hold the road but the intense fire from the militia and the King's Regiment forced them to retire. In the confusion most of the prisoners escaped from the enemy, but General Riall and William Hamilton Merritt were not among them.

As Merritt was marched past Forsyth's Tavern, he could hear the battle raging in the distance. Little did he realize the horror that the coming hours would bring.

Standing in their neat files, shoulder to shoulder, firing their ineffective volleys of musketry, Scott's brigade was slowly being cut to pieces. For forty-five minutes they fired and fell before the onslaught of the British artillery. Finally Scott ordered the brigade "to advance upon the enemy with a view to charge him." They had only marched a short distance however, when they were ordered to halt. They were now within four hundred and fifty yards of the British guns and standing on the farm lane that ran from the Portage Road, past the Peer Farm house to the lane leading to the Skinner farm (present day Drummond Road).

At 8:30, in the gathering darkness, Ripley's Second Brigade emerged from the chestnut grove to take its place in the line of battle. The second phase of the Battle of Lundy's Lane was about to begin.

To this point the British had had it all their own way with the exception of Jesup's attack on the left flank. The Glengarry Light Infantry, commanded by Lieutenant Colonel Francis Battersby, and elements of the Lincoln Militia with John Norton's warriors took advantage of Scott's advance to harass his left flank.

Lieutenant Colonel James Miller's Twenty-first U. S. Infantry moved forward in the darkness toward the British guns. Hidden by a thicket and the slope of the hill Miller intended to storm the British artillery from close range.

Lieutenant Colonel Joseph Morrison held his 89th Regiment of Foot below the brow of the hill on the north side of Lundy's Lane while the artillery pounded the American army. A sharp volley from the crest of the hill and the cries of wounded men galvanized him into action. He was about to order his regiment forward when the artillery horses, frightened by the sudden charge of the Twenty-First came crashing through the ranks of the 89th.

Morrison struggled to regain control of his troops losing precious minutes. After dressing the ranks the 89th unleashed a hail of musketry into the attacking Americans and charged. As they crossed the lane they encountered the little cemetery, which slowed their progress as they had to step around grave markers and artillery limbers. The 89th and the Twenty-First exchanged volleys at such close range that in places the muzzle flashes overlapped.

The Twenty-First and the 89th had met on the field of battle once before, at Crysler's Farm. At that time the Twenty-First retreated. Now it was the turn of the 89th who withdrew in good order from the hill.

Private Shadrack Byfield of the 41st Foot moved quickly into his place as the officers and sergeants checked the ranks as if they were on parade. Byfield had heard the sharp fire fight and assumed that the 89th was the unit involved. Whispers came down the ranks that the guns had been taken and they were about to recover them with a bayonet charge. He tried to moisten his lips, but his mouth was completely dry. The order came and they moved forward. Despite the darkness the ranks were kept, perhaps by instinct. Byfield loaded and fired successive volleys while men all around him fell, some screaming in pain, others silently, mercifully killed instantly.

Again the ranks fell back into the gloom. Shadrack Byfield marveled that he was unscathed. He thought it impossible that anyone could survive such an onslaught.

Lieutenant John Le Couteur of the 104th Foot watched in the gloom as the second attack returned. The 104th had been ordered to lay down out of harms way until they were needed. The commanding officer of the 104th, Lieutenant Colonel William Drummond of Keltie, was acting as a staff officer. Le Couteur saw him sitting on his horse with ball and shot whistling by his head. Suddenly a private of the regiment stood up and Le Couteur berated the man for disobeying an order in the middle of a battle to which the soldier, a Scot, replied, "Wall sir, de ye no see Colonel Drummond sitting on that great horse, up amongst all the balls-and sale I be laying down, sneaking whan he's exposed- Noe I wunt!" Le Couteur, who "could not but admire the fellow's generous heroism," left him alone.

Drummond, who was to have two horses shot from under him and his double barrel shotgun, which he usually carried into action, smashed in his hand during the battle, didn't suffer a scratch. Others did not lead the charmed life of William Drummond and casualties were heavy. Once more the Twenty-First held their ground and the British withdrew.

The battle raged in the growing gloom of night. The dense smoke hanging over the field added to the surrealistic images that ebbed and flowed in the flash of musketry. Friends were mistaken for enemies and fired upon. Enemies were mistaken for friends and allowed to pass.

The Americans consolidated their position on the hill. Contact between the two armies was temporarily broken as General Drummond reformed his division for another counterattack.

Confusion reigned supreme. Captain Thomas Biddle of the U.S. Artillery watched bemused as a British wagon pulled up to his position and unloaded its cargo of ammunition.

At 11:30 p.m. the British and Canadian forces, exhausted but determined, pushed forward in a third assault to regain their lost guns. It was at this point in the battle that Scott decided to move his shattered First Brigade back into action. Brown had ordered it into reserve on the arrival of the Second Brigade. Scott chose to attack the British in column rather than line and proceed to advance.

Inexplicably Scott passed between the Twenty-First and Twenty-third Infantry, wheeled left and passed between the American and British lines. The British were forming up for their counter attack when the shadowy figures of the First Brigade crossed in front of them. The U.S. Second Brigade saw them at the same time and poured volley after volley into their own troops. The British opened fire almost simultaneously with devastating effect. The Americans realized their mistake, but the damage was done.

The British advanced on the enemy. One of their volleys gave Jacob Brown a ball in the thigh. Brown rode forward but was struck by a ball in the left side nearly knocking him from his horse. The two armies closed with one another and the British halted within range and the exchange of volleys began all over again. The battle seesawed back and forth. The 89th got in amongst the guns and a violent struggle with the bayonet ensued. With the Royal Scots in support they engaged in vicious hand to hand combat in the smoke and darkness. Neither side was willing to give ground. Men slashed, stabbed and shot each other in a desperate bid to hold on to their slender grasp on the artillery.

For an instant the British were on the verge of victory, but the flanks began to withdraw and the centre followed. The third assault had failed.

It was at this juncture, about midnight, that a strange event occurred. Brown, urged by some of his officers, ordered the withdrawal of his army to Chippawa. After some debate the American retreated toward Chippawa leaving the captured guns on the field.

The next morning they advanced again, but finding the British in possession of the field withdrew, burning the mills at Bridgewater (Dufferin Islands) and the bridge across the Chippawa as they went. They retired all the way to Fort Erie.

CHAPTER TWENTY-EIGHT
THE CHESAPEAKE CAMPAIGN

While the British army under Drummond was preparing to follow the Americans and assault Fort Erie, another operation under Major General Robert Ross was in the planning stages. Ross was detached from Wellington's Army in Europe for service in North America. He sailed for Bermuda with three veteran regiments, the 4th, 44th and 85th where he was joined by three others bringing his total strength to forty-five hundred. In Bermuda the force fell under the overall command of Vice Admiral Alexander Cochrane, the new commander of the North American Naval Station.

The operation under discussion was a raid on Washington, the American capital. Oddly enough the impetus for this project could be traced back to the shores of Lake Erie in May of 1814. A raiding party of Americans attacked and destroyed the little village of Port Dover on Lake Erie. The marauders, under Abraham Markle, a lieutenant of Joseph Willcocks, burned every building between Port Dover and Turkey Point. The American high command quickly disavowed the act, but, Sir George Prevost was so enraged by this act of destruction that he asked Admiral Cochrane to help discourage any further atrocities.

Cochrane was happy to oblige. He wrote a letter to James Monroe, the American Secretary of State. It read in part: "Having been called upon by the Governor General of the Canadas to aid him in carrying into effect measures of retribution against the inhabitants of the United States for the wanton destruction committed by their army in Upper Canada, it has become imperiously my duty, conformable with the nature of the Governor General's application, to issue to the naval force under my command an order to destroy and lay waste such towns and districts as you may find assailable . . . .." After the burning of Niagara in December of 1813 the burning of Buffalo was considered sufficient retribution. After Port Dover destruction of private property became official British policy.

On 3 August 1814 Cochrane's subordinate, Rear Admiral George Cockburn, set sail with his fleet and Ross' army to attack the American capital. On 15 August the fleet entered Chesapeake Bay and two days later landed troops at Benedict, Maryland.

Benedict was empty as the landing barges released their cargo of redcoats. The streets of the little town were soon alive with four thousand British regulars, some foraging for extra rations as they formed up in three brigades for the march on Washington.

Eighteen year old Lieutenant George Gleig groaned as the bugle sounded assembly. He and his friend, Lieutenant Codd had managed to find three ducks and purchased a pig, a goose and some chickens from a farmers wife who had stayed on despite the invasion. They had just sat down to a feast fit for the king himself, when they were forced to abandon it.

The three brigades marched off toward their objective. In the sweltering heat of a Maryland summer many of the troops collapsed along the way. Ross was for canceling the whole enterprise, but Cockburn rode up and pressed him to go on.

Vice Admiral Cochrane also had misgivings about the chances of success and at 2:00 a.m. on the twentieth a courier woke up the two commanders with orders to withdraw. Cockburn insisted that success was assured and convinced Ross that they should proceed despite Cochrane's communique.

At the fork at Long Old Fields Ross hesitated. One road lead directly to Washington, the other swung to the right and approached the capital by a more circuitous route. Ross started up the direct road, but changed his mind, quickly reversing his column up the

road to Bladensburg.

The town was empty on their arrival. Surprisingly the bridges were still intact, but beyond, on the heights, the local militia was drawn up to give battle.

Things looked bad for the Americans. President Madison alerted his wife to be prepared to leave the presidential mansion at a moment's notice. He then rode out the Bladensburg Road with his cabinet to see for himself. He watched as the well disciplined British crossed the bridge under fire. Several officers went down in a hail of canister. George Gleig's friend, Lieutenant Codd, was killed on the Bladensburg Bridge.

Colonel William Thornton, commander of Gleig's brigade decided not to wait for the rest of the army and advanced on the waiting enemy. The light infantry attacked as a few Congrieve Rockets were fired. To say that Congrieve Rockets were inaccurate would be an understatement, but the militia had never seen them before. They broke almost to a man and ran from the field. The Battle of Bladensburg became known as the Bladensburg Races among the British officers.

The militia carried the second line of defence with them as they fled down the road to Washington. It now lay open to the advancing redcoats. The capital was abandoned and the rush to leave the city began. Dolley Madison waited as long as she could then cut Gilbert Stuart's portrait of George Washington from its frame and fled with the rest of the city.

Major General Ross and Admiral Cockburn rode into the city at the head of the 3rd Brigade. Sniper fire killed Ross' horse as they rode in. Ironically the shooting came from the house of Albert Gallatin, one of the American peace delegates at Ghent. The light companies of the 21st destroyed the building with Congrieve Rockets.

The British immediately went about the business of burning all the government buildings. The Capital was tough to fire as the lower floors were mostly of stone. The House of Representatives went up in smoke with desks, tables and chairs piled high in the domed chamber. The heat was so intense that marble turned to lime.

The Treasury Building was torched next followed by the Presidential Mansion. Here was found a table set for forty people in anticipation of a victory celebration. Cockburn toasted the Prince Regent instead and ordered the building burned. Even the general helped pile furniture in the oval office while a party of seamen replenished their torches at a nearby tavern.

The burning went on the next day with many private homes going up in flames. However many buildings were spared. Admiral Cockburn left one public building because several local women feared that their homes would be consumed in the ensuing fire.

The remarkable thing was the constraint of the British troops who mostly refrained from looting private property. Even Joseph Gales of the radical anti-British newspaper, the National Intelligencer, wrote: "Greater respect was certainly paid to private property than has usually been exhibited by the enemy in his marauding parties. No houses were half as much plundered by the enemy as by the knavish wretches of the town who profited by the general distress."

On 26 August Ross ordered his troops back to the ships and sailed up the Chesapeake to Baltimore. Here resistance was much stiffer and Ross was one of the British casualties. After two days of demonstration Cochrane set sail for Halifax.

Port Dover and, in the words of Sir George Prevost, the burning of the government buildings at York in 1813 was avenged. While these momentous events unfolded, the bloody siege of Fort Erie was underway.

CHAPTER TWENTY-NINE
THE SIEGE OF FORT ERIE

The Battle of Lundy's Lane was a costly one for both sides. The British counted five officers and seventy-nine other ranks killed, thirty officers and five hundred and twenty-nine men wounded and fourteen officers and two hundred and twenty-one men missing or taken prisoner. The Americans lost eleven officers and one hundred and sixty-two men killed, fifty-three officers and five hundred and seventy-one men wounded and eight officers and one hundred and nine men missing.

As the burial parties began their work it soon became apparent that they were fighting a losing battle against the heat that hastened the decomposition of the horses and men that littered the battle field. Sergeant James Commins of the 8th regiment described the scene on the morning of the 26th: "The morning light ushered to our view a shocking spectacle, men and horses lying promiscuously together, Americans and English laid upon one another, occasioned by our advance and retreat. . . .. It was found impossible to bury the whole so we collected a number of old trees together and burned them, which, although it may appear inhuman, was absolutely necessary and consequently justifiable."

One American officer who was buried was Captain Abraham Hull, son of General William Hull of Detroit fame. Another soldier who would remain forever on the hill by the road leading to William Lundy's farm was Ensign John Campbell of the Volunteer Incorporated Militia Battalion.

After his half-hearted advance on the morning of 26 July Ripley moved back to Chippawa and began arranging for the withdrawal to Fort Erie. The Americans burned the barracks and destroyed the earthworks on the north bank of the Chippawa. The bridge across the creek was also burned.

The wounded officers were placed in boats for the much easier trip by water to Buffalo. The enlisted men were loaded in forty wagons for the torturous land journey to Fort Erie. After the fit men took what they could carry the supplies from the wagons were dumped into the Niagara. It was at this point that Winfield Scott almost became a victim of the river. Because of the inexperience of the rowers, his boat was nearly swept over the falls.

At 3:00 p.m. the march to Fort Erie began. Another opportunity for a major American victory had slipped by. As they moved down the River Road they committed one last act of destruction. They burned the buildings on the farm of Samuel Street where they had won their victory at the Battle of Chippawa twenty-one days before.

The British were too exhausted to take advantage of the American flight toward Fort Erie. About the time that the American withdrawal was beginning Drummond sent his light troops and Indians forward to reconnoitre the enemy. The rest of his army he withdrew to Queenston. Holes in the ranks had to be filled and the troops resupplied before the pursuit of the enemy could begin.

On arriving on the shores of Lake Erie the Americans took advantage of the respite offered by Drummond to improve and expand the fortifications at the fort. Joseph Willcocks, one time member of the Upper Canada House of Assembly and now regarded as a turncoat, viewed the events of the last month with anger and frustration. The Americans had come within a hair of destroying the British army in the peninsula. He shuddered when he thought of Lundy's Lane and the horrors of fighting hand to hand in the darkness and the smoke. He knew now that his dream of living in a republican Canada was at an end. What galled him the most was that his neighbours, who had sneered at him when he had

prophesied the ultimate American victory, appeared to have been right. Exile in the United States was all that he had to look forward to now. He smiled, however, when he thought of the price he had extracted from his former neighbours for their insolence. They would long remember the name of Joseph Willcocks.

Willcocks and his Canadian volunteers threw their weight into the building of the new fortifications at Fort Erie. An American victory was their only chance to salvage something from the situation.

Finally, on 30 July, Drummond marched south with his army. He reached a point six miles from Fort Erie on 2 August where he made camp to plan his next move. Realizing that he had neither the men nor the materials

for a siege he ordered an attack on the American supply depots at Black Rock and Buffalo. He hoped that such action would force them to abandon the Canadian shore.

Private Shadrack Byfield of the light company of His Majesty's 41st Regiment of Foot stepped ashore in the darkness below Black Rock. He thought of Colonel John Tucker, commander of the 41st. He was always nervous when "Brigadier Shindy", as Tucker was called behind his back, commanded an attack.

True to form Tucker wasted four hours before advancing on the bridge over Conjocta Creek. When they arrived the Americans were alert and waiting.

Byfield approached the bridge in the

91

predawn light with the lead elements of the force. Suddenly a flash of musketry exploded from the far side of the creek and he felt his arm go numb before a burst of pain washed over him. Someone grabbed him and propelled him to the rear as his blood trickled to the ground. The 41st had broken under fire and retreated.

The attack was a fiasco and Tucker withdrew his troops back to the Canadian shore. Byfield waited patiently for his turn to see the surgeon. His emotions vacillated between the joy at being alive and the fear that he would lose his arm. Surgeon was doubtful but he did not remove the arm immediately. Shadrack made the painful journey to Fort George with the rest of the wounded.

Drummond was beside himself with anger and severely reprimanded the troops involved in the ill-fated expedition. He now was forced to contemplate a siege of the American position at Fort Erie.

By the time Drummond arrived before Fort Erie with his force on 4 August, the Americans had strengthened the fortifications to withstand the assault to come. The difficult task of constructing a siege battery began immediately. Lieutenants George Philpott and Joseph Portlock of the Royal Engineers chose a site near the lake north of the American position. The battery was completed on the 12th and armed with an 8 inch mortar, a 24-pdr. carronade and three 24-pdr guns. At daylight on the 13th the bombardment began.

The Americans had done their work well. The British siege guns were old and made little impression on the newly constructed earthworks. On the 14th a mortar shell exploded a magazine inside the fort and Drummond decided to attack that night. The siege of Fort Erie was about to take a bloody turn.

Captain James Kerby of the Incorporated Militia crouched in the early morning darkness, a feeling of foreboding scratching at his subconscious mind. It was 2 a.m., 15 August 1814 and Kerby was guiding the British assault troops toward their objective, the American battery at Snake Hill.

The plan of attack was complicated and to be carried out in complete darkness. The thing that disturbed Kerby the most was the order for all but a few men to remove the flints from their muskets. The assault depended on the bayonet alone to carry the position. The assault force consisted of the De Watteville Regiment, a newly arrived foreign corps, some men from the 8th and the light companies of the 89th and 100th.

As the force approached the objective the sky became alive with a wall of flame as the battery opened fire. The light revealed that the Americans had constructed an abatis of tree trunks bristling with sharp branches. In desperation the men attempted to out flank the position by wading into the lake. The enemy poured a steady fire into the flanking movement and as Kerby watched the De Watteville's broke and ran carrying with them the 8th. The only unit to stand firm was the 89th. In the muzzle flashes he could see that some had gained the parapet but their position was hopeless. Seeing the appalling casualties the commander, Lieutenant Colonel Victor Fischer of the De Watteville Regiment, ordered the withdrawal.

The other two columns fared little better. The Column led by Hercules Scott assaulted the breastwork with scaling ladders and were repulsed time after time. Scott himself was shot through the forehead and died shortly after. The column led by Drummond's nephew, Drummond of Keltie, managed to seize a part of the fort, but he too was killed. A short time later a violent explosion rocked the magazine in the north bastion and the British attackers were decimated. Those that survived, believing the entire fort to be mined, withdrew. The British losses were staggering. They had 900 officers and men killed, wounded and missing. In the incessant rain the wounded crawled or were carried to the makeshift field hospital where they were ministered to by the overworked surgeon and his assistants. More often than not a wound to a limb brought amputation as gangrene was

prevalent in the aftermath of battles.

The British and Canadian militia huddled in their miserable shelters while the rain turned their camp into a lake. Sickness was rampant and no regiment escaped as fever spread death through the ranks, killing as efficiently as any cannon or musket.

September 4th dawned gray and damp as Joseph Willcocks led a detachment of New York State Militia on a sortie against the British third battery. Willcocks was encouraged by the turn of events that had seen the British sustain heavy casualties in the fighting around Fort Erie. Perhaps his position could still be salvaged after all. Brown had 2800 men under arms and General George Izard was moving a further 3500 men to the theatre of operations in the near future.

The British fought to maintain their position against the American 21st Infantry as Willcocks' force approached. A Lincoln militiaman helping to the defend the battery with the regulars thought the leader of the American unit looked familiar, but he couldn't place him. He raised his musket to his shoulder, took aim at him and fired.

Suddenly, Willcocks roused himself from his musings. He raised his hand to halt the column just as a volley of musket fire erupted from the battery. Joseph Willcocks collapsed as the ball struck him. He lay on his back and caught a brief glimpse of sunlight breaking through the mist. Those eyes continued to stare into the sky long after the light had disappeared from them.

On September 21st Drummond bowed to

the inevitable and ordered the retreat back to Chippawa. The Americans had another glorious opportunity to wrest the peninsula from British control. With 6300 men under his command General Izard's prospects looked bright indeed.

The fates that had worked for the British and Canadians in the past stepped in once more to frustrate American designs. While camped on Street's Creek Izard learned that Commodore Chauncey had been driven from Lake Ontario with the launch of 102 gun HMS St. Lawrence. Izard wrote to the Secretary of War: "This defeats all the objects of the operations by land in this quarter. I may turn Chippawa and, should General Drummond not retire, may succeed in giving him a great deal of trouble, but if he falls back on Fort George or Burlington Heights, every step I take in pursuit exposes me to be cut off by large reinforcements. It is [now] in the power of the enemy to throw in twenty-four hours upon my flank or rear."

Izard did attempt to turn the British position at Chippawa. On the 18th of October he sent a force of 2000 to cross Lyon's Creek at Cook's Mills. Drummond immediately dispatched the Glengarry Light Infantry along with 7 companies of the 82nd Regiment to intercept them. On seeing the strength of the enemy the 100th Regiment was also sent with three more companies of the 82nd and one gun. The British force totaled about 750 all ranks. The Glengarries met the enemy at a ravine on the Matthew's farm and seeing that they could not dislodge the enemy by a frontal attack, withdrew a short distance drawing the Americans out of their defensive position. A short, sharp exchange resulted in the Americans retreating from the field after burning the grain stored there.

This was the last skirmish of any con-sequence in the peninsula. Izard ordered the withdrawal of all forces to Fort Erie, which he mined and blew up before crossing back over to the American shore.

Although the peninsula was now back in British hands the area was so desolate that it was open to raids by marauders who would sweep down on isolated farms. One company of the Glengarries under Fitzgibbon of Beaverdams fame was stationed at Turkey Point to engage these raiders where possible.

With the announcement of peace in March 1815 the pioneer settlers of the Niagara Peninsula started to rebuild their lives and heal the wounds of three years of bitter warfare.

HISTORICAL NOTES: Captain James Kerby had originally been adjutant of the 2nd Regiment of Lincoln Militia and had joined the Volunteer Incorporated Militia Battalion in March of 1813. He was involved in partnership with Robert Grant operating warehouses at Queenston for goods traveling on the Portage Road.

Shadrack Byfield's left arm was amputated and he left us an account of the procedure. He wrote: "They prepared to bind me, and had men to hold me; but I told them there was no need of that. The operation was tedious and painful, but I was able to bear it pretty well. I had it dressed, and went to bed. They brought me mulled wine, and I drank it. I was then informed that the orderly had thrown my hand to the dung-heap. I arose, went to him, and felt a disposition to strike him. My hand was taken up and a few boards nailed together for a coffin, my hand was put into it and buried on the ramparts. The stump of my arm soon healed, and three days after I was able to play a game of fives, for a quart of rum."

EPILOGUE

The War of 1812 was a watershed in the history of Upper Canada and the Niagara Peninsula. The first stirrings of nationhood rippled through the scattered communities of British North America. Canada was conceived on the battlefields of 1812-14. The gestation period was to be fifty three years, but after a long, hard labour our country was born on July 1, 1867.

We live in a time when the very survival of Canada as a nation is in doubt. We as Canadians are questioning our identity as a people. It is important that we seek out the answers.

Just as in families, we know who we are by looking to our parents and our parents' parents; so too as a society we discover who we are by those who went before us. In the history of our country lie the answers to the questions that plague us.

Our neighbors to the south's heroes become larger than life. We Canadians have always understated our achievements and hesitated to blow our own horn because it was "too American." However, we must put aside our natural reluctance and find ourselves in the heroic deeds of our forbearers. Nowhere in Canada can this be better accomplished than right here in the Niagara Peninsula. There is more history per square metre here than anywhere else in the country.

The settlers who came to this part of Canada in the late 18th century were, for the most part, loyalists who fought on the British side during the American Revolution. They came from well established farms in the new United States to begin again in the pristine wilderness that was Niagara. They laboriously cleared the land and built rough, one-room log cabins for their families. They struggled to raise food to feed themselves as well as supply the garrison at Fort Niagara. Famine struck in 1789 reducing many to eating their dogs and horses. Yet these forbearers of ours persevered. By the early 19th century they began to prosper, regaining some of the relative luxury they had been forced to abandon in the United States.

From 1800 to 1812 many of the settlers who came here were Americans lured by the promise of free land and a new life. For an oath of allegiance and a promise to work the land, grants or land for purchase at reasonable prices were available in some prime agricultural areas such as Niagara.

The War of 1812 brought the age of growth and prosperity to a screeching halt. The loyalists who had once fought against American republicanism were asked again to take up arms to thwart their ambition to drive the British from North America.

As we have seen the Peninsula became one of the major battle grounds of the war. It began with the Battle of Queenston Heights and ended with the Battle of Cook's Mills in present day Welland. Between these two battles American troops burned and pillaged their way from Fort Erie to Newark (Niagara-on-the-Lake).

The Canadian Volunteers, serving in the American Army and lead by Joseph Willcocks, took revenge on their former neighbors, burning farms and running off livestock. The most notable incident occurred at midnight on December 10, 1813. The Americans burned Newark, leaving the inhabitants without shelter. They also destroyed St. Davids in July 1814. Newark was avenged by the capture of Fort Niagara and the burning of everything from there to Buffalo. St. Davids resulted in the cashiering of the American officer responsible by an enraged General Brown commanding the American forces.

When peace finally came in March 1815 the Peninsula was in a shambles. Newark was

in the process of being rebuilt, St. Davids was in ashes and many farms were in ruins. Much of the land was untillable due to the ravages of war. Some would never work their farms again for they were casualties of the many skirmishes and battles the militia engaged in.

Local heroes and heroines sprang up to answer the call. The most famous, Laura Secord, made her famous trek to Beaverdams to warn the British of an imminent attack. Her uncle by marriage, Major David Secord, of the 2nd Lincoln Militia, had fought as a young man with Butler's Rangers in the American Revolution. He answered the call once again, commanding the regiment at the Battle of Chippawa after his Colonel was wounded. General Riall praised the conduct of the Regiment in a dispatch printed in the London Gazette dated August 9, 1814: "The conduct of the officers and men of this Regiment has also been highly praiseworthy."

Sixteen members of the 2nd Lincoln Militia were killed in this battle. Most of them were from Stamford Township. Some of their names are familiar to us today: Forsythe, Hill, Peer, Skinner and Thompson, among others.

William Hamilton Merritt will always be remembered as the builder of the Welland Canal, but we rarely hear of his exploits during the war. Merritt was a captain in the Troop of Provincial Dragoons, the militia cavalry unit. He was a dashing cavalry officer, chasing American irregulars and harassing foraging parties in true hit and run fashion.

Twelve hours a day in the saddle were

common for Merritt and his troopers. He fought in many of the major battles of the war; Queenston Heights, Stoney Creek and Lundy's Lane among them. At the latter he was taken prisoner and spent eight months in an American prison.

In the volume that follows we will pick up the history of the Niagara Peninsula in 1815. We will look at the triumphs and tragedies of the people who had to rebuild their lives. The Welland Canal will be a prominent part of our narrative as it changed forever the destiny of all who call Niagara their home.

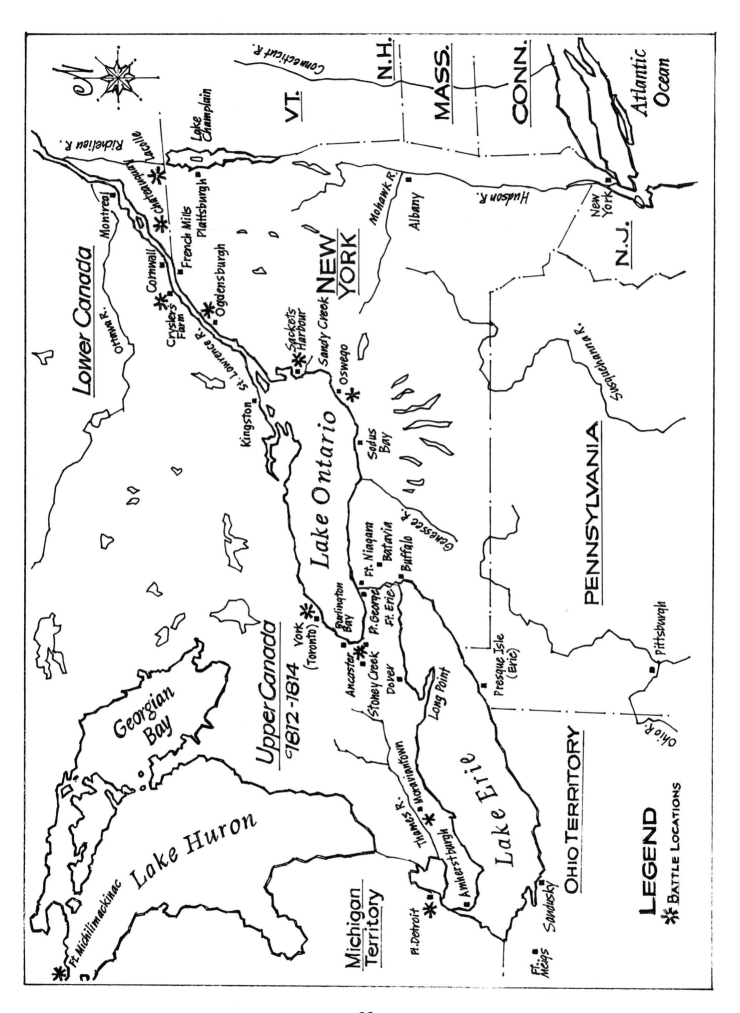

N

Lower Canada

Montreal

Ottawa R.

Richelieu R.

Lacolle

Châteauguay

Cornwall

Crysler's Farm

St. Lawrence R.

French Mills

Ogdensburgh

Lake Champlain

Plattsburgh

VT.

N.H.

Connecticut R.

MASS.

CONN.

Atlantic Ocean

Mohawk R.

Albany

Hudson R.

New York

N.J.

NEW YORK

Sandy Creek

Sackets Harbour

Oswego

Kingston

Sodus Bay

Lake Ontario

PENNSYLVANIA

Susquehanna R.

Genessee R.

Batavia

Ft. Niagara

Buffalo

Burlington Bay

York (Toronto)

Upper Canada
1812-1814

Ft. George

Ft. Erie

Ancaster

Stoney Creek

Dover

Long Point

Presque Isle (Erie)

Pittsburgh

Ohio R.

Georgian Bay

Lake Huron

Ft. Michilimackinac

Thames R.

Moraviantown

Amherstburgh

Michigan Territory

Ft. Detroit

Lake Erie

Sandusky

Ft. Meigs

OHIO TERRITORY

LEGEND
✳ Battle Locations

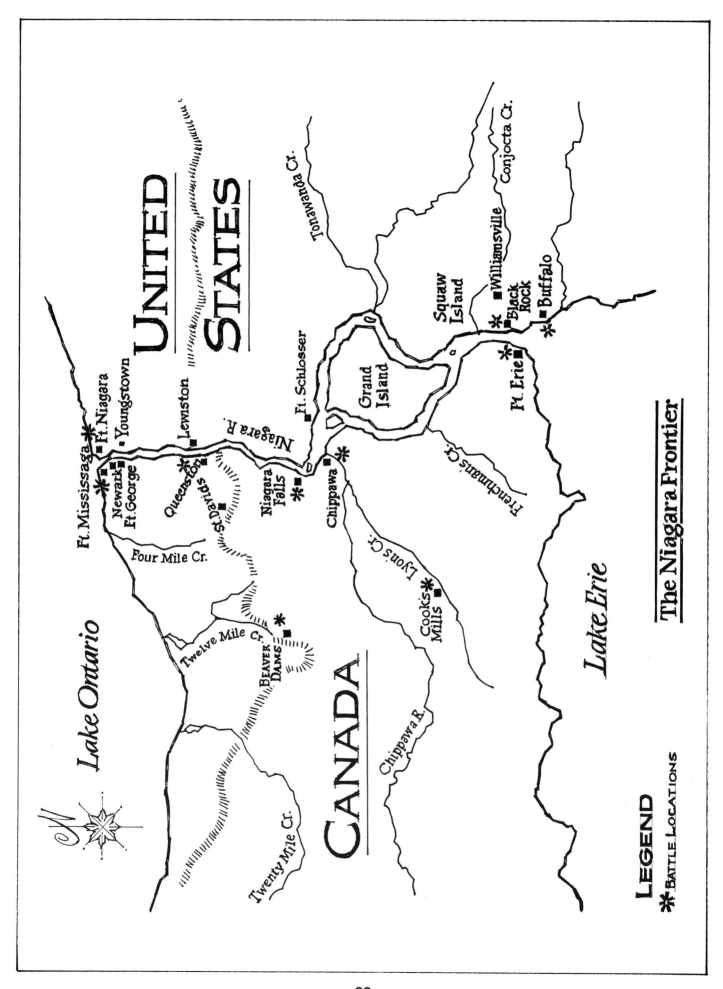

The Niagara Frontier

LEGEND
✴ BATTLE LOCATIONS

INDEX